THE GREAT SWAN
ON THE WING;
THE FLIGHT
OF THE ALONE
TO THE ALONE.

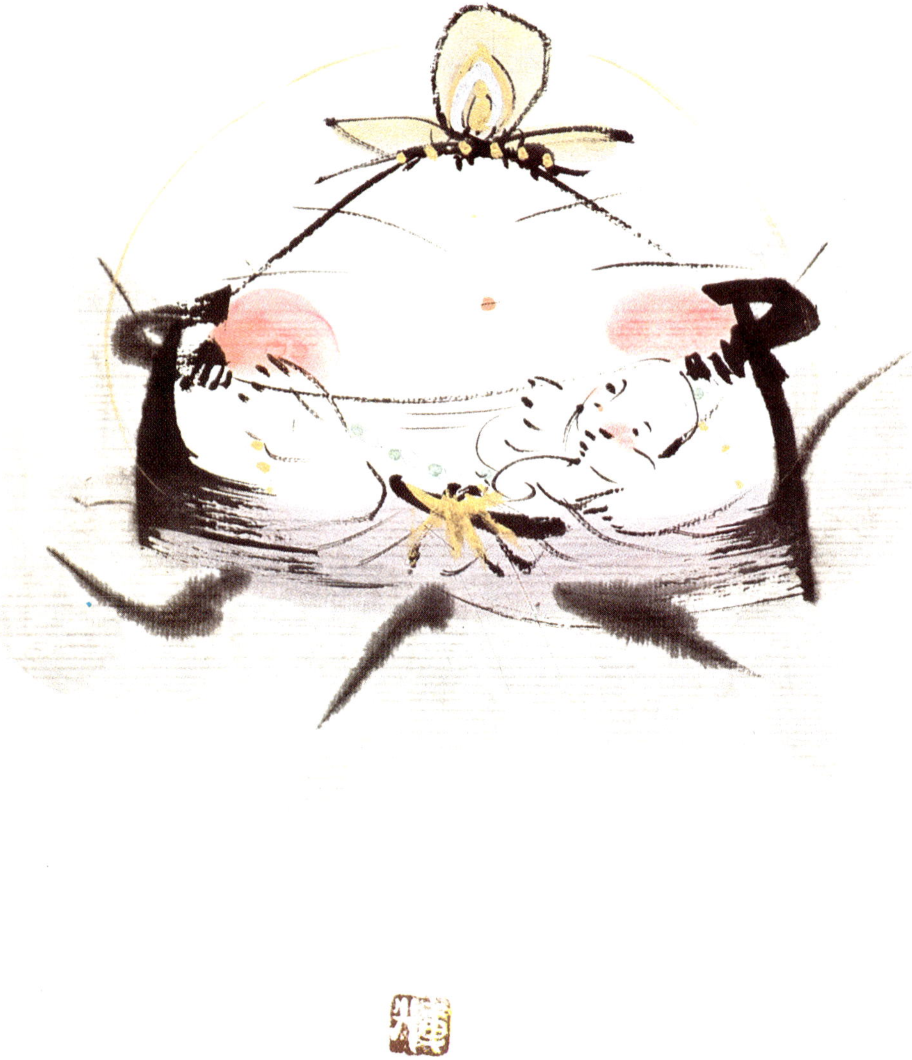

THE
REBEL
PUBLISHING
HOUSE

Editing by Ma Deva Sarito
Swami Anand Robin, M.A. (Cantab)

Typesetting by Ma Prem Arya

Design by Swami Shivananda, M.F.A.

Paintings of "The maiden Avalokitesvara"
by Teruo Kanno, Kobe, Japan
Painting of "The great swan on the wing"
by Ma Prem Prartho, B.A., M.A.
Other paintings by Ma Anand Meera
(Kasué Hashimoto), B.F.A. (Musashino Art University, Tokyo)

Calligraphy by Ma Prem Mansha; Ma Deva Satyama
Swami Anand Govind, Dipl.-Ing.

Production by Swami Prem Visarjan; Swami Prem Prabodh
Swami Satyam Ambhoj, M.A.; Swami Prem Joshua

In loving gratitude to Osho Rajneesh
Rajneesh Foundation Australia

Printing by Mohndruck, Gütersloh, West Germany

Published by The Rebel Publishing House GmbH
Cologne, West Germany

Copyright © Neo-Sannyas International

First Edition

All rights reserved

No part of this book may be reproduced or transmitted in any form or by any means electronic or mechanical including photocopying or recording or by any information storage and retrieval system without permission in writing from the publisher.

ISBN 3-89338-060-4

Talks given to the
Rajneesh International University of Mysticism
in Gautama the Buddha Auditorium, Poona, India
December 26, 1988 – January 7, 1989

Dedicated to Katue Ishida, seeress and prophetess of one of the most ancient shrines of Shinto in Japan, Ise shrine, with great love and blessings.

大なる愛と
祝福をこめて
日本最古の神社の一、
伊勢神宮の
見者にして預言者なる
石白カツヱ女史に
捧ぐ

NO MIND

THE FLOWERS OF ETERNITY

OSHO RAJNEESH

Table of Contents

1	To Create a Few More Rainbows	2
2	An Assembly of Two Buddhas	18
3	A Meeting of Two Rivers	42
4	In Your Eyes is the Hope of the World	62
5	I Am Just Myself	78
6	My Change has Taken Me Higher	92
7	The World of the Gurus has Ended	112
8	Truth Has No History	136
9	Be Ready to be Chopped	160
10	When I Call You My Friends, I Mean It	182
11	Only Creation Shows Your Power	200
12	Nothing to Choose, Nothing to Discard	228
13	You Need Two Wings	258

Introduction

This book chronicles a twelve-day revolution in the life of Osho Rajneesh beginning on December 26, 1988, a period which altered the lives of millions of people – and most of them don't know it.

Life has its strange ways, but this was the strangest. The Living Master, Osho Rajneesh, in a sizzling retort to thirty years of accusations and abuse about His name 'Bhagwan', dropped it altogether.
The explanation He gave of His simple strategy – to adopt and then drop the name 'Bhagwan' – dealt a paralyzing blow to two of the so-called "great religions" of India, Hinduism and Jainism. The name was a challenge they could never meet, created by a man they could never equal.

It revealed a secret which even the Master's most intimate disciples never knew. He *showed* something which could never be uttered; a Master stroke was needed.
One man against 900 million people, and the solitary man had won.

The third "great religion" born in India, Buddhism, then had its share of attention. For millions of Buddhists worldwide, the haunted wait for the return of Buddha's soul was over. As predicted, the 'Maitreya', the reincarnated soul of Buddha, had come – and had chosen as his home none other than Osho Rajneesh.

What happened in the next four days puzzled Buddhist pundits, scholars and theologians the world over – and defeated the expectations of everyone. The Master exposed a forgotten but obvious truth: that truth itself is fresh, never old, never antique. And the whole idea of Gautama the Buddha as a returning guide is anachronism, a bullock cart in the space age.

The very dream of a return to some imagined perfection of the past, He showed, could keep us from living the sweetness of *this* moment, from living the benediction of our *own* buddha nature. Another burden removed.

He showed us in these twelve discourses that this moment contains an even greater possibility than Gautama the Buddha promised, a different and greater synthesis, a vaster discovery: Zorba the Buddha.

Osho Rajneesh became that. Explained that. And moved on. He left a wild unexplored space behind, a space for His disciples, a promise, a potential. Wild flowers blooming on the slopes of Everest. Springtime.

Swami Dhyan Yogi, M.D.

Note to the Reader

The end of each discourse in this series follows a certain format which might be puzzling to the reader who has not been present at the event itself.

First is the time of Sardar Gurudayal Singh. "Sardarji" is a longtime disciple whose hearty and infectious laughter has resulted in the joke-telling time being named in his honor.

The jokes are followed by a meditation consisting of four parts. Each stage of the meditation is preceded by a signal from Osho to the drummer, Nivedano. This drumbeat is represented in the text as follows:

The first stage of the meditation is gibberish, which Osho has described as "cleansing your mind of all kinds of dust… speaking any language that you don't know …throwing all your craziness out."

For several moments, the hall goes completely mad, as thousands of people shout, scream, babble nonsense and wave their arms about.

The gibberish is represented in the text as follows:

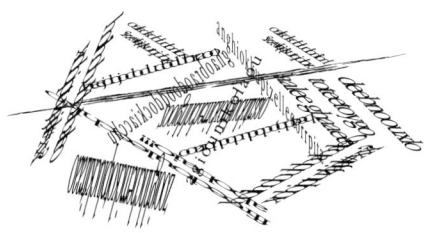

The second stage is a period of silent sitting, of focusing the consciousness on the center, the point of witnessing.

The third stage is "let-go" – each person falls effortlessly to the ground, allowing themselves to dissolve the boundaries that keep them separate.

A final drumbeat signals the assembly to return to a sitting position, as they are guided in making their experience of meditation more and more a part of everyday life. The participants are guided through each stage of the meditation by the words of the Master, and the entire text of each evening meditation is reproduced here.

Every night is an occasion for celebration at Rajneeshdham, as sannyasins and friends gather in Gautama the Buddha Auditorium to wait for the evening discourse.

At about 6:45pm the musicians begin to play, softly at first, and as the time for the Master's arrival draws near, building the tempo. The music reaches a crescendo several times, each time climaxing in a roar of "Yaa-Hoo!" – arms raised to the sky, a pindrop silence, and then the music slowly begins again.

In the stillness following the last and mightiest "Yaa-Hoo!" the Master appears on the podium, hands folded in the traditional Eastern greeeting of *namaste*. The assembly returns His greeting, bowing down as His gaze travels slowly over each part of the hall.
Finally the Master takes His seat, the music stops,
and the discourse begins.

To Create a Few More Rainbows
December 26, 1988

Beloved Bhagwan,

Once a monk was asked by Kyōzan, "Where have you come from?" to which the monk replied, "From Yushu."
Kyōzan then asked him, "I'd like to know something interesting about Yushu; what's the price of rice there?"
The monk replied, "As I was coming here, I unintentionally passed over the bridge of that town and trod on the girders of the bridge, breaking them."

On another occasion Kyōzan was washing his clothes and Tangen asked him, "What should we do at this moment?"
Kyōzan answered, "At this moment where shall we look?"
Tangen made no reply.

At another time Kyōzan saw a snowman and, pointing to it, said to the group of monks around him, "Is there anything whiter than that?"
His monks were unresponsive.

My Beloved Ones, I have been too long away from you. But this "awayness" was just like the glasses I'm wearing. Although you cannot see me, I can see you.

I used to hear your "Yaa-Hoo." And each time I heard it stars showered over my small hut.

These few days and nights have been days and nights of a certain purification. The poison that has been delivered to me by President Ronald Reagan and his staff...from all over the world experts in poison said that amongst all the poisons this is the one which cannot be detected in any way. And it has been the practice of the CIA in America to give this poison, because there is no way to find it out. And if you cannot find it you cannot give any antidotes. Death has been almost certain.

These long days and nights I have taken the challenge of the poison, just witnessing. The poison was a constant torture on every joint of the bones, but a miracle has happened. Slowly slowly, from all joints it has disappeared. The last were the two arms. Today I am free from that too.

I have a strong feeling that although I was not physically present here, you have felt me in the air. You have felt me more closely than ever before. And in your songs, I was present. In your meditations, remember, I was more present than physical presence allows.

I had to come out today for a special reason.

A few months ago in Bombay, Govind Siddharth had a vision that Gautam Buddha's soul has been searching for a body. And he saw in his vision that my body has become a vehicle for Gautam Buddha.

He was right. But this is the misfortune of man: that you can go wrong even though you had touched upon a point of rightness. Because I declared him to be enlightened, he has disappeared. Since then I have not seen him. Perhaps he thinks, "Now, what is the use? I was searching for enlightenment and I have found it."

Enlightenment is only the beginning, not the end. He came very close and has gone very far away.

But I was waiting for the recognition from a Zen source that Gautam the Buddha is trying to use my words and my silences, my heartbeats and my inner sky to create a few more rainbows, to spread a few more flowers in the world. That recognition has come from a very famous seeress and prophetess from Japan.

One of our sannyasins was there. He could see the sincerity of the woman. She never praises anyone; her insight is clear. He was afraid to ask about me, but finally he decided to ask and without any hesitation she said, "I was waiting for a messenger. You have come at the right time. Gautam Buddha is using Bhagwan's body.

"Right now take these twenty-one very precious real pearls as a present to Bhagwan with my congratulations that a soul that has been wandering around in search of a vehicle has found it."

The sannyasin was a little doubtful, because he said, "Bhagwan's body has been poisoned in America. Will Gautam Buddha accept a vehicle which has been poisoned?"

The sincerity of the woman reminds me of Almitra of Kahlil Gibran's *Prophet*. She said, "Have you ever heard that a Satan or a devil has been poisoned? It has been the destiny of the Buddhas. Don't think that the body has become impure by poisoning. This has been a fire test, and Bhagwan has come out of it. You take these pearls and my message, and I will be coming myself to pay my respects."

By the way, I have been calling myself "Bhagwan" just as a challenge to this country, to the Christians, to the Mohammedans, to the Hindus. They have condemned me, but none has been courageous enough to explain the condemnation. From faraway sources there have been articles and letters sent to me saying, "Why do you call yourself Bhagwan?" And I have laughed, because why does Ram call himself Bhagwan? Is he appointed by a committee? And a Bhagwan appointed by a committee will not be much of a Bhagwan, because the committee does not consist of Bhagwans. What right have they?

Is Krishna elected by the people as Bhagwan? Is it an election matter? Who has appointed these people? No Hindu has the answer. And a man like Krishna has stolen sixteen thousand women from different people – they were mothers, they were married, unmarried – with no discrimination, and yet no Hindu has the courage to object that a man with such a character has no right to be called Bhagwan.

They can call Kalki, a white horse, "Bhagwan." Strange people! And they ask me why I call myself Bhagwan. I don't have any respect for the word. In fact I have every condemnation of it. It is not a beautiful word – although I have tried in my own way to transform the word, but the stupid Hindus won't allow it. I have tried to give it a new name, a new meaning, a new significance. I have said that it means the Blessed One, a man with a blessed being, although it was my invention.

The word 'bhagwan' is a very ugly word. But the Hindus are not even aware of it. They think that it is something very special. Its root meaning – *bhag* means a woman's genital organs. And *wan* means a man's genital organs. The meaning of the word 'bhagwan' is symbolically that he brings about in the feminine energy of existence, through his male chauvinistic energy, the creation.

I hate the word! I have been waiting for some Hindu idiot to come forward, but they think that it is something very dignified and I have no right to call myself Bhagwan. Today I say absolutely, "Yes, but I have every right to denounce the word." Nobody can prevent me. I don't want to be called Bhagwan again. Enough is enough! The joke is over!

> *I don't want to be called Bhagwan again. Enough is enough! The joke is over!*

But I accept the Japanese Zen prophetess. And from now onwards I am Gautam the Buddha. You can call me "The Beloved Friend." Drop the word 'Bhagwan' completely. Even very intelligent people, people who respect me and love me...

Just the other day I received an appreciation of my book *Zarathustra* by an internationally famous journalist. He has praised it, and he has said that after Adi Shankara – the most famous Hindu philosopher – I am the second as far as intellectual, rational, spiritual authenticity is concerned.

But still he could not forget the word 'bhagwan', why I called myself Bhagwan. But does he know that he is comparing me with Adi Shankara who has been called for over a thousand years "Bhagwan Adi Shankara." And nobody asks the question why.

Anybody would be happy to be compared with Adi Shankara, but I am not. It is not a compliment to me, because Shankara is the reason that Buddhism, which was a higher flowering, was destroyed – by Shankara and the Hindu priesthood. I cannot accept that Shankara has any genius. He is orthodox, just trying to protect the investment of the Hindu priesthood, which is the world's worst, the ancientmost rotten priesthood.

I refuse to be compared with this man, particularly because he was the reason the roses were destroyed that Gautam Buddha had managed to grow in the soil of this land. In my eyes he is a criminal of the worst kind.

But as far as Gautam the Buddha is concerned, I welcome him in my very heart. I will give him my words, my silences, my meditations, my being, my wings. From today onwards you can look at me as Gautama the Buddha.

I will tell you about the Japanese Buddhist seeress – she has sent her picture:

"Katue Ishida, mystic of one of the biggest and most famous Shinto shrines in Japan, stated recently after seeing Bhagwan's picture, that: 'This is the person that Maitreya the Buddha has entered. He is trying to create a utopia in the twenty-first century. Lots of destructive power is against Him, and some people call Him Satan. But I have never known Satan to be poisoned. He is usually the poisoner, not the poisoned. We must protect this man, Bhagwan. Buddha has entered Him.'"

With great love and respect I accept Ishida's prophecy. She will be welcome here as one of my people, most loved. And by accepting Gautam the Buddha as my very soul, I go out of the Hindu fold completely; I go against the Jaina fold completely.

I have seen and condemned everything that was happening but was not in favor of the Hindu monks, Jaina monks. I have been consistently condemning celibacy as one of the most unnatural acts. Now two Jaina monks have come with their own autobiographies, renouncing the Jaina fold and declaring that behind celibacy all kinds of sexual perversions are prevalent.

Young women are persuaded to become nuns. The family feels fortunate that their daughter has been accepted as a nun, and also financially it is good. In India for a girl to be married is the worst calamity that can happen to a family. But if a girl is accepted as a nun the whole family becomes in a certain way holy. And these nuns are exploited sexually.

I have been in contact with nuns and monks, and they have in privacy accepted that, "You are right, but our problem is we are not educated. If we leave the monkhood the same people who touch our feet are going to kill us or at least are going to reduce us to beggars on the streets."

NO MIND: THE FLOWERS OF ETERNITY

The Hindu Acharya Tulsi has been trying to get the government to prohibit these two books that have just been published, because he himself is implicated in homosexuality. In fact if the Indian government had any guts the first thing would be to require that all the monks – to whichever religion they belonged – should be examined thoroughly, because most probably their perversions of centuries have brought the AIDS positive. That seems to be their only positive contribution to the world!

Maneesha's sutra:

Beloved Bhagwan...
You will have to learn, Maneesha, not to call me by that ugly name again. I am just your friend. That's what Gautam Buddha's prophecy was: "My name after twenty-five centuries, if I can find a vehicle, will be Maitreya Gautam Buddha." Maitreya means the friend. From now onwards you will have to change your old habit.

I am your Beloved Friend. You can call me "Beloved Buddha," which simply means the awakened one. But we have to spread around the earth that I have denounced "Bhagwan." I have in fact, just one day, taken it on myself to denounce it. I don't have any rights on it, but I have every right *not* to call myself Bhagwan.

The sutra:
Once a monk was asked by Kyōzan, "Where have you come from?" to which the monk replied, "From Yushu."
Kyōzan then asked him, "I would like to know something interesting about Yushu; what is the price of rice there?"

These are special devices of Zen. Kyōzan is provoking the monk by asking this question; he is asking whether he remembers the past, which is no more, the village of Yushu and the price of rice there. But the monk proved equal to Kyōzan.

As Kyōzan asked, "I would like to know something interesting about Yushu; what is the price of rice there?"...

The monk replied, "As I was coming here, I unintentionally passed over the bridge of the town and trod on the girders of the bridge, breaking them."

This is an old, very ancient saying of Buddha, that when you pass a bridge, break it, because there is no way of going back.

On another occasion, Kyōzan was washing his clothes and Tangen asked him, "What should we do at this moment?" Kyōzan answered, "At this moment, where shall we look?"

Kyōzan is saying, "Just find out if there are any bridges connecting you with the past and break them. Be independent of the past, just be here and now in this moment."

Except *this* there is no Zen, no Gautam the Buddha, no religion, no essential and existential experience of life, of love, of this tremendous cosmos. Just be disconnected from the past and be disconnected from the future. Being in this small and still moment you are also the buddha.

Tangen made no reply.

Tangen making no reply is a way of accepting a failure.

Kyōzan is washing his clothes, neither in the past nor in the future, just herenow; there is no Kyōzan, there is only washing of the clothes.

At another time Kyōzan saw a snowman and, pointing to it, said to the group of monks around him, "Is there anything whiter than that?"
His monks were unresponsive.

WHERE
THERE ARE HUMANS
YOU WILL FIND FLIES,
AND BUDDHAS.

They could not understand that what Kyōzan is asking has nothing to do with snowmen; they are all imaginary. But he is saying, "If there is a snowman" – he must be pure white, snow white – "is there anything whiter?"

There is! Your very being. Nothing can be whiter, more luminous than your own very existence.

Issa wrote:
Where there are humans
you will find flies,
and buddhas.

This whole cosmos consists of everything. If you find human beings you will find flies. Issa is saying, "To find buddhas amongst you is as simple as finding flies." Buddha does not put himself in any superiority game. Buddha breaks down all the games that have been invented by all the traditions and the religions – the games around God, the games around hell, the games around virtue, the games around sin, all are simply man-made games. Buddha simply wants you to be completely free from man-made projections.

Just be simple and here. Let the stars shower on you and let the lotuses blossom in your being. You are not beggars, you are carrying all the splendor of existence within you; you have just not looked in.

Buddha has brought religion to its very essential simplicity. That's his contribution; against all traditions, against all stupid superstitions, he has rebelled.

If I am accepting him, to use my hands as his gestures, it is only because of his rebelliousness. Of course I am going to refine his rebelliousness – in twenty-five centuries, too much dust has gathered. Behind the dust the mirror is absolutely clean.

Maneesha has asked:
We have heard You have been very sick. Would You like to talk about it?

No, Maneesha. Being sick is enough. To talk about it is being more sick. And remember, my body can be sick, I am never sick. I watch everything, whatever happens. I will watch my death as I watched my life, and that's my simple teaching to you.

Before Sardar Gurudayal Singh...
These glasses are for great Avirbhava.

(He holds out his glasses and motions Avirbhava to the podium. Totally surprised, and characteristically overcome, her flustered response delights the whole assembly into laughter and applause.)

Yes, great, put them on! Everybody wants to see.

Judy comes back from her honeymoon and is gossiping with her friend, Diane.

"Well?" Diane inquires. "How was your honeymoon night?"

"Oh, Diane!" Judy exclaims. "It was horrible. All night – up and down, in and out, up and down, in and out. Never get a room next to the elevator!"

Edgar and Louisa Snodgrass are Christian missionaries in Africa. They have been taken prisoner by the local cannibal tribe and are standing in a huge cauldron filled with water. Both are frightened beyond belief. Suddenly, Edgar starts giggling.

"What on earth are you laughing about at a time like this?" Louisa asks with a shocked expression.

"Those bastards don't know it yet," Edgar snickers, "but I just pissed in their soup!"

A Smutz Beer official is naming the winner of the Smutz Beer slogan contest on national television.

"And the winner is Herbert Fine, for his winning slogan: 'Smutz Beer – like love in a canoe.'"

Fine walks up to the stage and receives the ten thousand dollar bill. The official shakes Fine's hand and says, "That's a wonderful slogan, Mr. Fine. Please, tell our national audience why you feel that Smutz Beer is like love in a canoe."

"Sure," says Fine. "It is like love in a canoe because it is fucking close to water!"

Now, Nivedano...

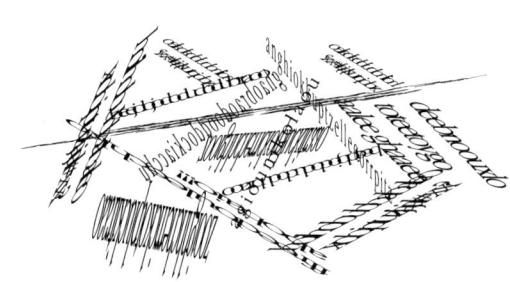

Nivedano...

NO MIND: THE FLOWERS OF ETERNITY

Be silent. Close your eyes. Feel your body to be completely frozen.

Now look inwards with your total consciousness and with an urgency as if this is the last moment of your life.

The totality of consciousness and such urgency is bound to bring you to the very source of your being.

Suddenly you have disappeared from the circumference and you are sitting deep at the center like Gautam the Buddha.

Flowers are showering,
a new breeze,
a fresh fragrance,
an open sky full of stars,
a sense of eternity.
To know this is all there is to know.

To make it clear,

Nivedano...

Relax. Just be a witness of the body and the mind. You are not the body, you are not the mind, you are just a pure watcher, a witness. This witnessing is the very essence of existential religion.

This is not a mere teaching, this is Gautam Buddha's sharing, his own experience of the eternal, giving you freedom from the body and the mind. The Buddha Auditorium suddenly has become a lake of consciousness; personalities have disappeared, there is not even a single ripple in the lake.

Collect as much oceanic experience as possible. You have to bring the buddha back with you. You have to live the buddha in your everyday experience.

Nivedano...

Come back, but come back like buddhas, with the same grace, with the same joy. Just sit for a few minutes to recollect where you have been, who in fact you are.

Okay, Maneesha?
Yes, Buddha.

An Assembly of Two Buddhas
December 27, 1988

Beloved Buddha,

On one occasion when a monk asked Kyōzan the meaning of Bodhidharma coming from the West, Kyōzan drew a circle in the air and put the character for Buddha inside it.
This left the monk without words.

At another time, Kyōzan was living in Sekitei Temple in Kōshu. A monk came up to him and said,
"Master, do you know Chinese characters?"
"As far as befits my position," responded Kyōzan.
The monk then circled Kyōzan once in the anti-clockwise direction and asked him, "What character is this?"
Kyōzan drew the character for the number ten.
Then the monk walked around him in a clockwise direction and asked what character that was.
Kyōzan changed the figure ten (which looks like a plus sign) into a swastika.
The monk then drew a circle and pretended to hold it in both his hands and asked Kyōzan, "What character is this?" at which Kyōzan drew a circle around the swastika.
The monk then pretended to be Rucika, the last of the one thousand Buddhas of the present kalpa, at which Kyōzan commented, "That is right! That is what all the Buddhas have kept – you also, I also. Take care of it!"

Maneesha, I am feeling so light, just by dropping a single word. I feel I can fly like a swan to the eternal snows of the Himalayas. That small word I had chosen as a challenge to this country's whole past. For thirty years I carried that word.

There are so many Hindu scholars, shankaracharyas, Jaina monks – none of them had the courage to challenge me on the word. Perhaps they were aware that to challenge me on the word would be an exposure of the whole Hindu structure of society, which is the ugliest in the world.

But the man who wrote the *Manusmrati* five or perhaps seven thousand years ago is still ruling the Indian mind. He was called Bhagwan Manu, because he gave the morality and the character to Hindu society. The Hindu society is one of the most spiritually enslaved societies. Its slavery is in its caste system. The caste system is the ugliest you can conceive. It also labels the woman as an inferior creature, spiritually incapable of being enlightened.

Gautama the Buddha rebelled against the caste system; that was his great crime.

In his presence it was impossible to argue with him. He was not a man of argument but of existential presence. Scholars, pundits, brahmins approached him, but his very climate was enough to silence them. They did not have courage enough to question this man's single-handed rebellion against the most ancient society in the world. Just because of this, I see Gautam the Buddha as the only man in the whole past of human history who knew what freedom is.

Yesterday you witnessed a historical moment.

I have accepted Gautam Buddha's soul as a guest, reminding him that I am a non-compromising person, and if any argument arises between us, "I am the host, and you are the guest – you can pack your suitcases!" But lovingly and with great joy he has accepted a strange host – perhaps only a strange man like me could do justice to a guest like Gautam the Buddha. Twenty-five centuries ago he was the most liberated, but in twenty-five centuries so much water has flowed down the Ganges. It is a totally new world of which he knows nothing.

With great respect he will have to depend on me to encounter the contemporary situation.

He understood it immediately. His clarity of vision has remained pure all along these twenty-five centuries. I am blessed to be a host of the greatest man of history. And you are also fortunate to be a witness of a strange phenomenon.

When Gautam Buddha died, the brahmins, the priesthood which has been a curse to this country, destroyed everything that Buddha had created. All those beautiful roses were burnt alive. There were three categories of people: those who were enlightened simply left the country to convert the whole Far East; those who were not enlightened either suffered death or were forced to become part of the *sudras*.

It was one of the great contributions of Doctor Ambedkar to discover that the *chamars,* the shoemakers, are really Buddhists who have been reduced to shoemaking by the Hindu priesthood. With their lives at risk, the poor fellows preferred this utter humiliation and indignity. But Buddhism disappeared completely from its own land.

You will not believe how revengeful the priesthood is.

They burnt the Bodhi tree under which Gautam Buddha had become enlightened; even the tree could not be tolerated. The tree that exists now in Bodhgaya is not the original tree. It was just a coincidence that before the original tree was destroyed by the brahmins, a great emperor, Ashoka, became interested in Gautam Buddha and his awakening. He is the only great emperor who lived like Buddha's bhikkshus, who begged his food in his own capital.

He cut a branch of the original tree and sent his own daughter, Sanghamitra, to Ceylon to plant the tree and to plant the seeds of Buddha's great awakening in Sri Lanka.

Just after India became liberated, Jawaharlal Nehru, the first prime minister of this country, was in immense love with Buddha. He asked that a branch from Sri Lanka should be brought back. It is a faraway descendant of the original tree under which Gautam Buddha became enlightened, but yet it carries the same juice.

So the tree you see now in Bodhgaya is not the original tree. The original has been burned. Such is the revengeful attitude of all priesthood around the world.

I wanted the Hindu priesthood to challenge me on the word 'Bhagwan'. But knowing me perfectly well, they simply avoided the challenge because it was going to expose all their incarnations of god.

You will not believe what kind of criminals have been called "Bhagwan" by Hindus.

As an example I would like to tell you: Parasuram is one of the incarnations of a Hindu god. His old father, according to the Hindu scriptures, was a great seer. But I don't think that is right, because a great seer will not be suspicious of his wife. A great seer transcends all these small desires and longings, jealousies. I will call that man, not a seer, but one of the blindest of people because he was suspicious that when he goes to the river early in the morning in the dark, the Moon God comes to have a love affair with his wife. Such idiots!

The moon is not a god; it is just a piece of this planet. But he ordered his son, Parasuram, "Until you cut off the head of my wife, your mother, my suspicion and my jealousy will go on burning like fire in my heart."

Parasuram, without asking, "What are the reasons for this jealousy? A man like you is not supposed to be jealous, and in your old age..." he simply went and cut off the head of his own mother. Just because of his obedience to his father, howsoever irrational and stupid, Hindus have called him "Bhagwan." I never had any desire to belong to this category of criminals.

Yesterday, dropping that word, I have disconnected myself with this land, its ugly heritage, its slavery.

One friend has asked if it was a mistake when I referred to Tulsi as Hindu, or do I mean it. I'm not any infallible pope, but that was not a mistake; I mean it.

Jainism never could become an independent religion. It depends for all its necessities on Hindus. It is only a philosophy, not a religion; a Hindu cult, but not a culture. No Jaina would be ready to make shoes; no Jaina would be ready to clean toilets. What kind of culture is this? It is simply a small branch of the Hindu heritage, maybe differing on a few philosophical points, but that does not make it a religion. So, with absolute awareness I called Acharya Tulsi a Hindu.

The people that Hinduism has been worshipping as gods... It is so hilarious! Krishna is worshipped as the perfect god and he is the man who forced this country into the greatest war India has ever known. It was an unnecessary massacre. It left Hindu society without a spine. It became so afraid of war that it has been available for anybody to invade it.

For two thousand years it has remained a country enslaved by small barbarian tribes – this vast continent – but nobody wanted any violence. The mind of the whole country settled into the consolation of fatalism: "If somebody is coming to invade – Moguls, Hunas, Turks, Mongols, anybody – this is destiny, you cannot avoid it. It is better to accept it; it is destined by God." That's why even after the freedom from the British empire, forty years have passed, and one wonders what we had asked freedom for.

Freedom has two wings – from and for. A freedom that is only "from" is not worth the name. Freedom has to be for something greater.

But India continues to become more and more poor, more and more uneducated. And the stupid politicians promised the country, "We are going to lead you into the twenty-first century."

The country is not even in this century. It still lives according to Manu, seven thousand years back; it still worships Krishna, five thousand years past. It seems all that has to happen has happened for this land. It has no future; its dark night has no dawn.

By dropping the word 'Bhagwan' I have disconnected myself absolutely from an ugly tradition – inhuman, barbarious. It has created a mind for slavery, uncreative in every sense, and in the name of spirituality every kind of nonsense goes.

Gautam Buddha fought like a lion. I am immensely happy that he has chosen me. His area of fight was very small, just the state of Bihar in North India; my field of work is the whole world.

I have to fight not only against the Hindu superstitions, I have to fight with the Mohammedans, with the Christians – alone, but with great rejoicing, hoping that the courageous ones are going to join my caravan.

The fight is at the most crucial time. The world cannot be saved. These coming twelve years are going to be the last for this beautiful planet to breathe, to blossom into flowers. My work and yours is to find the chosen people before the idiotic politicians destroy the world. Let us create as many buddhas as possible because they will be the only ones whose bodies may be destroyed but whose souls will have wings to fly across the sun into the blue sky and dissolve into eternity with joy, with dance, with gratitude.

Maneesha has brought a few beautiful sutras.

Beloved Buddha,
On one occasion when a monk asked Kyōzan the meaning of Bodhidharma coming from the West...

It is a traditional question containing many implications: "Why did Bodhidharma come from India to China?"

Certainly the first implication is that India was no longer receptive to the highest flight of consciousness of Buddha. Bodhidharma was in search of fresh ground, of new pastures.

Kyōzan drew a circle in the air and put the character for Buddha inside it.

Without saying a word, just making a circle in the air and putting the Chinese character for Buddha inside it…not a single word is spoken but everything is said, including that which cannot be said in any way. He is indicating that life is like a circle in the air, very fragile. Like a writing on the sands on the beach, and a tidal wave comes and takes away all the writing or a wild breeze comes and disturbs everything that is written.

Kyōzan is saying that your life is even more illusory, just a circle in the air; you cannot even see it. But inside the circle a tremendous force of consciousness, represented by the Buddha, is hidden in all its splendor.

Bodhidharma coming to China was carrying the message, "Don't just waste your life on the circumference, which is nothing but a circle drawn in the air. Look inwards. Always remember that the difference between life and death is not much – just a few breaths, a few heartbeats missed, and you are no more in the body. But inside, in this ephemeral circle of air is the very solid, immortal rock of the Buddha." Bodhidharma went to China to carry the message to which India had become absolutely blind and unreceptive.

This left the monk without words.

He could see the great insight of Kyōzan.

At another time, Kyōzan was living in Sekitei Temple in Kōshu. A monk came up to him and said, "Master, do you know Chinese characters?"
"As far as befits my position," responded Kyōzan.

I have to remind you that Chinese or Japanese or other Far Eastern languages don't have any alphabet. They have only characters. It is very difficult to understand those languages unless you are born there because you need to know thousands of characters to read even an ordinary newspaper, and those characters are very symbolic.

One friend showed me a Chinese character. I tried in every way to work out what this character could be but I had to accept failure. The man said, "It is a very simple character, but unless you know there is no way to discover it."

It is just a symbolic roof with two symbolic women. Neither can you figure out that these are women and this is the roof... And the man told me, "This character means constant quarrel: two women under one roof; but it also means battle, fight, war."

He had been learning Chinese for almost thirty years, but he was still not confident about the ancient scriptures.

So when the monk asked, "Do you know the Chinese characters?" Kyōzan responded, "As far as befits my position. I cannot say I know Chinese characters, I can only say I know a few characters which are needed for my work."

The monk then circled Kyōzan once in the anti-clockwise direction and asked him, "What character is this?"
Kyōzan drew the character for the number ten.

One wonders – why number ten? Moving around you anti-clockwise, why should it mean ten?

I have tried hard. My own understanding is, all the languages of the world have ten digits as the basis of their mathematics, and those ten digits come from the ten fingers of man.

Man started counting on his fingers. I still do! And howsoever hard I try, at the most I reach to the third finger. By the time I reach the fourth I have forgotten whether it is fourth or fifth....

This character within an anti-clockwise movement can simply mean that you will be limited to the small numbers – up to ten. You cannot go further than that. If you want to go further you will have to move clockwise – that is how existence is moving. Anti-clockwise, you will be stuck with your own fingers.

Kyōzan drew the character for the number ten. Then the monk walked around him in a clockwise direction and asked what character that was.

Kyōzan changed the figure ten (which looks like a plus sign) into a swastika.

The swastika is, perhaps, the ancientmost symbol in the world. It moves clockwise.

When Adolf Hitler came to power, he wanted for his flag some ancient symbol. He sent his messengers to India, to Tibet, to China, and they all came to the conclusion that the swastika is the ancientmost symbol in the world. It means progress, it means being in tune with existence, it means victory. But the people who had brought this message from the eastern countries made the flag for Adolf Hitler, but forgot to make the swastika clockwise. They made it, but because it was unknown to them they made it anti-clockwise.

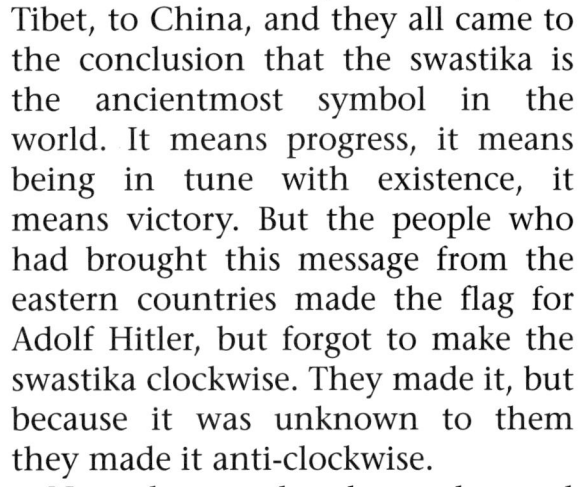

Now the people who understand numerology, symbology, say that Adolf Hitler's defeat is because of this wrong swastika character on his flag. I will not go along with them; that is nonsense. Clockwise or anti-clockwise is not going to decide the fate of a war.

But Kyōzan is right in the sense that if you are in tune with existence, you may have the possibility of your potential coming to a flowering. Don't go against the current; that way your defeat is certain. Go with the current; that way you are relaxed, joyful, floating with the stream, and you will reach to the ocean – to the vast oceanic consciousness.

NO MIND: THE FLOWERS OF ETERNITY

The monk then drew a circle and pretended to hold it in both his hands and asked Kyōzan, "What character is this?" at which Kyōzan drew a circle around the swastika.

The swastika is the symbol of time, clockwise. But time is nothing but a mind projection. If there is no mind, there is no time. Do you think the bamboos around the Buddha Auditorium know anything about time? Do you think the sun rises according to a clock? The whole existence goes on without having any sense of time. Time is a projection of the human mind. Except in your watches and clocks there is no time.

Kyōzan did well. He drew a circle in the air around the swastika – that too is in the air. He is saying, all that our mind can do is made of the same stuff as dreams are made of.

TO WAKE, ALIVE,
IN THIS WORLD.
WHAT HAPPINESS!
WINTER RAIN.

The monk then pretended to be Rucika, the last of the one thousand Buddhas of the present kalpa, at which Kyōzan commented, "That's right!"

This is the Buddhist mythology: that every kalpa means millions of years in which a world is born and dies – that is one kalpa. This earth was born four billion years ago, and it seems we have most probably twelve years more. There is every indication that by the end of this century we are going to commit suicide.

AN ASSEMBLY OF TWO BUDDHAS

In this whole kalpa there are one thousand buddhas, and Rucika, mythologically, is thought to be the last buddha of the present kalpa.

The monk then pretended to be Rucika, the last of the one thousand Buddhas of the present kalpa, at which Kyōzan commented, "That's right! That is what all the Buddhas have kept – you also, I also. Take care of it!"

The only thing to be taken care of is your innermost being, symbolized by the buddhas. Lose everything and you lose nothing. Empires disappear in the air like soap bubbles. But don't lose your buddha. That is your eternal treasure, your immortality, your master key to open all the mysteries of existence.

Shōsha wrote:

To wake, alive,
In this world.
What happiness!
Winter rain.

Just suddenly in winter, when it is not expected, comes a rain cloud, and showers create so many rainbows.

Shōsha is saying,
"To wake, alive,
In this world, where everything is mortal –
what happiness! Winter rain."
Every morning when you wake up, remember it.

I have come across a man, well-educated, a retired professor of mathematics, who suddenly became very much afraid of sleeping. His family brought him to me. They said, "He is absolutely rational in everything except he does not like to sleep. Moreover, he goes on waking others in the family."

He would knock on the doors of his daughter-in-law, "Are you awake?" Now, just to answer him her sleep is disturbed. But the whole night...what else can he do?

I asked him, "What is the fear? Why don't you want to sleep?"

He said, "The fear is that if I go to sleep, what is the guarantee that I will wake up alive."

I said, "This is certainly a very significant problem. But who told you that you are alive?"

He said, "I am not alive?"

I said, "As far as I can see you have been dead since you retired. You can sleep; you cannot lose anything, you are dead already."

He said, "That solves the problem. All these people have been bothering me: 'Sleep!' but nobody could give the right answer. You convinced me. If I am dead already, who cares?"

I went to see him the next morning. He was taking his breakfast. He welcomed me with great love and said, "It is a miracle! I awakened alive."

And I said, "Remember, if you don't sleep you will be dead. If you sleep there is a possibility you may wake up alive."

After twenty years I went back to the city. He had become very old, and he said to me, "Now I have come with a very different question: I want to die."

I said, "Sleep well. One day it is certain, I can guarantee you will not wake up. The best place to die is in bed. Ninety-nine percent of people die in bed. That is the most dangerous place."

He said, "My God! I have been sleeping on a bed."

I said, "You start sleeping on the mattress down on the floor."

He said, "What is that going to do?"

I said to him, "Remember, there is no way to avoid death. You can make every effort, and the best thing is not to go to bed. The bed is very close to the cemetery."

I have heard about an old Jew who was dying, a very rich man. His four sons were discussing: "The old fellow is going to die. What to do about the funeral procession?"

The youngest son said, "He always wanted to have a Rolls Royce. The poor fellow could not manage it, not because he did not have the money, but it was impossible to part him from his money. Once he had got hold of it, then that money could not be used in any way. But we can have for his funeral procession a Rolls Royce – at least once, a one-way drive. He will not come back."

The second son said, "Don't be stupid. What does it matter to a dead man whether he is riding the Rolls Royce or just a bullock cart. An unnecessary waste! You are too young, you don't understand."

The third son said, "So you propose a bullock cart. My feeling is: we are four, we can carry him on our shoulders. The cemetery is not far away."

The old man was listening to everything. He suddenly sat up in the bed and said, "Where are my shoes?"

One son said, "Shoes? Are you going to die with your shoes on?"

He said, "No. I simply want my shoes, because I am still alive enough to walk down to the cemetery! Listening to the great discussion that is going on, the cheapest way is..."

But whatever you do, Shōsha is right:

To wake, alive – again –
In this world.
What happiness!
Winter rain.

Maneesha has asked:

Beloved Buddha,
Gautama the Buddha died by poisoning. You have survived in spite of being poisoned. Is there any connection between the two? Is there a particular significance in the timing of Your declaration that Gautama Buddha is living on in You?

Maneesha, it is true Gautam Buddha died of poisoning. The fact is, he was too old, eighty-two years old, and tired. Forty-two years just walking from village to village... He could not fight back against the poison. But his work was incomplete.

In fact the work of a buddha is always going to be incomplete. It is an intrinsic part of spreading the fire of awakening. You cannot conceive that the whole world will become awakened, but people like Gautam the Buddha are the dreamers of the impossible. They hope against hope. He had to leave because his body was tired and old and could not survive the poisoning. But he left with a dream that he may

AN ASSEMBLY OF TWO BUDDHAS

find somewhere someone to carry on his dream of growing more lotuses in the world. These twenty-five centuries he has been wandering like a white cloud, searching.

It is my great destiny that he has chosen me to be his host. I will do – in fact I have been doing already – the same kind of work of spreading awakening. Hence it is not a problem to me. An ancient buddha residing inside will certainly strengthen my work.

You are asking about poisoning, "Is there any connection?" Certainly, seeing that I have overcome the poisoning, which was far more dangerous than the poisoning that Buddha suffered. The poisoning has been a great purification for me. This purification makes me receptive to the wandering soul of Gautam Buddha.

He is not a weight. He is rather more like wings. He is not the man to dictate anything – the pure agnostic, the greatest individualist, the utter rebel. I have been, without knowing, preparing a home, a shelter, for a wandering Buddha. It is my fortune that he has accepted me to be his home for a few days at least.

You are also fortunate to be the assembly of two Buddhas, a bridge stretched between twenty-five centuries, so rich that if you miss, nobody except yourself will be responsible for it.

It is time for Sardar Gurudayal Singh. Gautam the Buddha may not be aware…because I don't find in his scriptures any sense of humor. But now in this assembly even a dead man will start laughing.

Polanski, the Polack, applies for a job at the Poona Travel Agency. He tells them that he worked three years for Polish

Airways. The personnel director calls Polish Airways to see what kind of an employee Polanski was.

His previous boss says:

"He is a meathead, a cheat, a dumb bunny, a busybody, a loafer, a birdbrain, a sneak, a numbskull, a loudmouth, a fruitcake, a dodo, a chiseler, a bigot, a wino, a lamebrain, a dunce, a boob, a bananahead, an ass, a screwball, a dumb-dumb, a nincompoop, a goofball, a dimwit, a pig, a hockey puck, a klutz, a dummkopf, a fuddy-duddy, a ding-a-ling, a lush, a weirdo, a dunderhead, a moron, a bungler, a mental midget, a turkey, a bloodsucker, a bully, a muttonhead, a slavedriver, a vulture, an imbecile, a tightwad, a dingbat, a braggart, an animal, a puttyhead, a bitcher, a clown and an idiot! Still, I recommend him for the job."

"Why on earth would you recommend him?" asks the personnel director.

"Because," the previous boss says, "he was our best employee!"

Hymie Goldberg is lying on the psychiatrist's couch.

"So what seems to be the problem?" the shrink asks.

"Well, Doc," Hymie replies. "For the past two months, every morning at eight-thirty, I take a huge shit!"

"Really?" says the psychiatrist, after a moment's silence. "Why, millions of people would love to be that regular. So, what is the problem?"

"Well, Doc," Hymie replies, "I don't get out of bed until nine!"

Marco is a newcomer to the country. Although he does not know the language well, he manages to meet Janet and dates her for several weeks. Then, Janet invites Marco to her house for dinner. When he arrives Janet excuses herself and goes off to the kitchen to help her mother. Marco gathers up all his courage and says: "Sir, I wanna ask for your daughter's gland."

"What?" cries the father. "You mean you want my daughter's *hand?*"

"No," says Marco. "I'm fed up with hand jobs. Now I want the gland!"

The quiz show moderator says to the contestant, "Okay, Mr. Clump, and now, for the one hundred thousand dollar question, what is the difference between Ronald Reagan and a bucket of shit?"

Clump thinks for a second, then smiles knowingly and declares, "The bucket!"

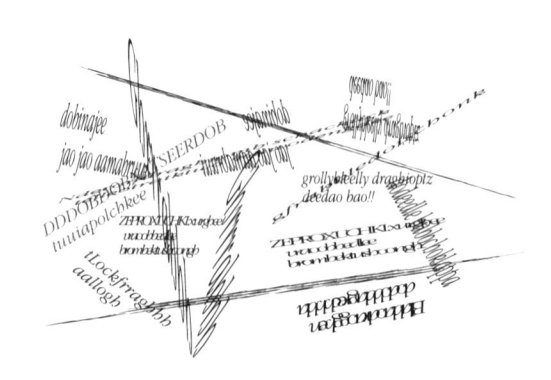

Nivedano... ((((-))))

Nivedano... ((((-))))

Be silent. Close your eyes. Feel your body to be completely frozen.

Now look inwards with your total consciousness, and with an urgency as if this moment is going to be the last in your life.

The center of your being is not far away. As you come closer, a strange coolness, a silence starts becoming deeper. A light that has no source, a blissfulness…thousands of flowers start raining on you.

This moment, you are the buddha.

This is your ultimate reality. The only character to be remembered is witnessing. The buddha consists only of witnessing.

To make it clear,

Nivedano…

Relax, and just be a witness. You are not the body, you are not the mind. You are just a pure witness standing by the side. This witnessing is the very soul of a buddha.

The night was beautiful in itself, but ten thousand buddhas melting into an oceanic consciousness has made the night a splendor, a miracle.

Just remember one thing: when Nivedano calls

you back, gather as much light, as much
fragrance, as much existential juice as you can,
and persuade the buddha to come along with you.
Finally, he has to become your everyday action,
gesture, word, silence – everything.
The circumference of your life has to disappear,
giving place to the center.

This is the greatest rebellion and the only living
religiousness: to bring buddha into your ordinary
life, simply, innocently.

Nivedano...

Come back...with all the grace of a buddha,
with all the beauty and the joy. Sit for a few
minutes just to recollect the golden path that you
traveled to reach to your center, and the
encounter with the buddha, and the experience of
just pure witnessing.

Slowly slowly, that which looks like a faraway
peak of consciousness will become your simple,
ordinary being. That will be the most historical
moment for you.

Okay, Maneesha?
Yes, Buddha.

A Meeting of Two Rivers
December 28, 1988

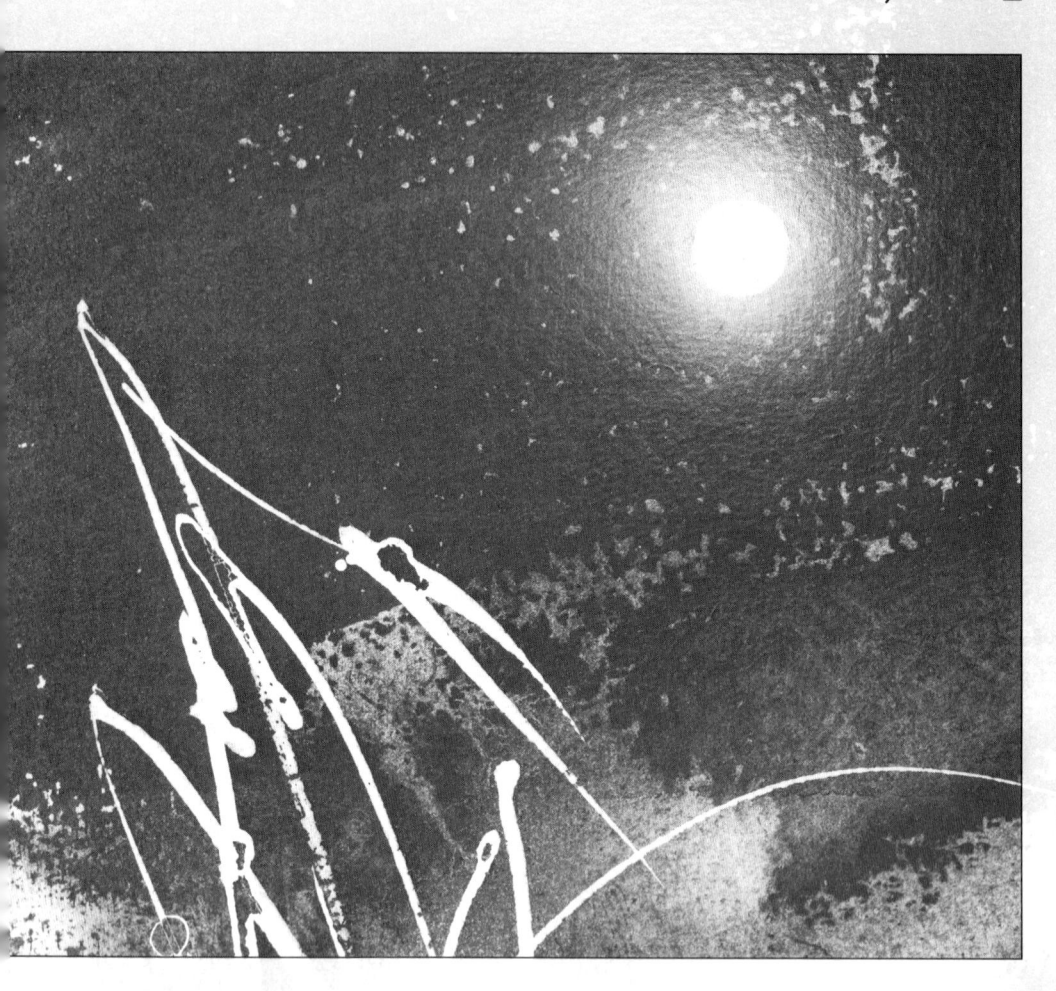

Beloved Buddha,

Once Kakusan went to see Kyōzan. Raising his foot, Kakusan said, "The twenty-eight Indian Patriarchs were like this, and the six Patriarchs of the Country of T'ang were like this, and *you* are like this, and *I* am like this!"
Kyōzan came down from the Zen seat and hit him four times with the wisteria staff.

After Kakusan became enlightened, an ascetic once said to him, "What is the true meaning of Buddhism?"
Kakusan remained silent and bowed to him.
The ascetic asked, "Are you bowing to a man of the world?"
Kakusan replied, "Don't you see what I am saying? I am your famous disciple!"

At another time Kyōzan, on seeing a monk approach him, raised his mosquito flapper. At this, the monk shouted loudly, "Kwatz!"
Kyōzan commented, "There *is* such a thing as saying 'Kwatz,' but tell me, where was my mistake?"
The monk replied, "In improperly pointing to an external object" – at which Kyōzan hit him.

Maneesha, the new situation, the new responsibility that I have taken upon myself has raised many questions from different quarters. Perhaps it will take a little time to clarify any questions, doubts, suspicions or mere curiosities.

The first thing is from the chief of staff of United Press International. He has sent a telegram asking me, now I have allowed Gautam Buddha to be my guest, have I become a Buddhist? In the same reference he has asked: "What about your followers? Are they also now part of an organized religion? Have they also become Buddhists?"

The question is absolutely relevant, but my answer may baffle the chief of staff of UPI.

Gautam the Buddha has taken shelter in me. I am the host, he is the guest. There is no question of any conversion. I am a buddha in my own right, and that is the reason he has felt to use my vehicle for his remaining work. He has been waiting, a wandering cloud for twenty-five centuries, for a right vehicle.

I am not a Buddhist. Neither is Gautam the Buddha's intention to create Buddhists, or to create an organized religion. Even twenty-five centuries before, he never created an organized religion. The moment truth is organized it becomes a lie. An organized religion is nothing but a hidden politics, a deep exploitation by the priesthood. They may be shankaracharyas, imams, rabbis, or popes, it makes no difference.

Gautam Buddha did not leave behind him any successor. His last words were, "Don't make my statues, don't collect my words. I don't want to become a symbol which has to be worshipped. My deepest longing is that you will not be imitators. You don't have to be Buddhists because your own potential is to be a buddha."

I would like to say: I don't teach Buddhism, or any 'ism' for that matter. I teach the buddha himself. The people who are with me are not part of any organized religion. They are independent, individual seekers. My relationship with them is that of a fellow traveler.

By the way, I have to remind you of Gautam Buddha's prophecy twenty-five centuries ago: "When I come again I will not be able to be born through a woman's womb. I will have to take shelter in a man of similar consciousness and the same height and the same open sky. I will be called 'The Friend.'"

A tremendous freedom is implied in the word. He does not want to be anybody's guru, he simply wants to be a friend. He has something to share, with no conditions attached to the sharing.

The moment truth is organized it becomes a lie.

This also will help you, because a few sannyasins have been confused how they will make the difference between the ancient Gautam Buddha and me. Gautam Buddha's prophecy helps to clarify the confusion.

Although he has taken shelter in me, I will not be called Gautam the Buddha. I will love to be called according to his prophecy: Maitreya The Buddha. 'Maitreya' means the friend. That will keep the distinction. There will not be any confusion.

As far as I am concerned, I have always been against any

organized religion. My love, my longing is to create as many individuals in the world as possible, utterly independent, in absolute freedom of their soul, no fetters of Christianity or Hinduism or Mohammedanism. No scriptures, no teachings …no discipline except a self-awareness, a flame burning in your very soul, making you aware and alert and a witness.

There is a small community of Buddhists in Maharashtra. They are Buddhists newly converted by Doctor Babasaheb Ambedkar. These are the untouchables whom Hindus have been exploiting for centuries, humiliating them utterly disgracefully. These are the most oppressed, exploited, humiliated human beings upon the earth.

But Babasaheb Ambedkar could not convert all the untouchables, who are one-fourth of the Hindu fold. He himself was not a meditator. His effort to convert the untouchables into Buddhists was in order to take them out of the Hindu fold, so they can gain their dignity as human beings. This was a political step, a social revolution, but it has nothing to do with spirituality.

I have received a message from that small community that Doctor Ambedkar converted, hoping that perhaps I will give them an organized religion. I am sorry to say, the very word 'organization' is irreligious.

I do not teach religion, I teach religiousness – a quality, not a membership of any church but a quality that transforms your being, brings the flowering of your potentiality.

Those Buddhists who have been left in a kind of darkness and in difficulties, I am available to help them not to be Buddhists but to be buddhas. Less than that is below my comprehension. I want a world full of buddhas, absolutely free to fly in the open sky.

A MEETING OF TWO RIVERS

Truth brings freedom, meditation brings freedom – freedom from scriptures and freedom from the words of the ancients. It brings a silence, a peace, and a sense of eternity, immortality, deathlessness. It brings a dance to your life, a new song, a new music, a new way of living in grace and love. But it has nothing to do with any organized religion.

All organized religions have proved criminals, murderers. They have done nothing but massacre. They have burned living human beings all over the world. If we want a new world, we have to get rid of all organized religions. Religiousness is just like love. Have you ever heard of organized love?

It reminds me....

Just the other day in England the Duke of Edinburgh made a very strange statement. In the parliament they were discussing curtailing hunting because so many species of animals are simply disappearing.

The Duke of Edinburgh is a well-known hunter. He did not agree with the parliament, and he said, "There is no difference between hunting and purchasing meat from a butcher's shop." And to give an example, perhaps not knowing its implications, he said, "The difference between hunting and purchasing meat from a butcher is the difference between a married woman and a prostitute, and there is no difference between a married woman and a prostitute." The parliament was shocked.

They have prevented me from entering England, but I have my own ways of entering...! I have been saying this again and again for three decades, that there is no difference between marriage and prostitution. Marriage is a little longer contract, prostitution is a shorter contract. Both are purchased with money.

But he did not think it through. What does it mean? Queen Elizabeth is a prostitute? England is ruled by a prostitute? But it is true! And prostitution will be dropped only if marriage disappears. Prostitution is a by-product of marriage, and while marriage remains there is no way to avoid prostitution.

For centuries, every society has tried to destroy prostitutes, but they don't understand that it is a by-product. No by-product can ever be destroyed. Can you destroy your shadow? Your shadow is simply a by-product.

Marriage creates a bondage, and every bondage creates a tremendous desire to have a little freedom at least once in a while. That freedom creates the prostitutes.

But why keep all the women either as slaves in the name of marriage or as prostitutes? It is so ugly, so barbarious. Just drop marriage and let every woman be utterly free and independent.

Love cannot be purchased, and if you purchase it, it cannot be love. You can love out of freedom, and your love should enhance the freedom. If it destroys freedom it is committing suicide itself.

One sannyasin has asked: "Now you have disconnected yourself absolutely and categorically from the Hindu fold and the Jaina fold, in fact, from the whole past of this country. Will you still be criticizing Hindus and Jainas?"

Of course. Now my sword will be sharper, and my hammer will be bigger. In fact, I have disconnected myself absolutely from any fold, any organization for this very purpose. And on my own I am not going to create any organization. That will be against my very being, against my whole life's effort.

My love is freedom, and those who have gathered around me – and many more will be coming – they have to remember it. You are not becoming a member of any church. You are just joining hands with friends who are traveling on the same path. At any moment you can leave the path. Everyone is welcome to join, and everyone is welcome in freedom, with blessings, if he wants to go to seek somewhere else.

I bless all kinds of seeking on all paths.

Before the sutras, a little biographical note:

Kakusan was a disciple of Kyōzan. After his enlightenment he lived on Mount Kaku from which his name is derived – Kakusan.
When he was about to die, Kakusan collected a pile of firewood deep in the forest. At noon he refused his meal, went to the pile of wood, lit it and climbed on top.
Kakusan then put his umbrella behind his head to make a halo. Thus he ended his life in the flames, holding out his staff like the demon-subduing vajra.

Standing, he died in the fire. It must have been a very strange sight: when the fire cooled, he was still standing – utterly burned, dead, but holding his staff straight. That staff has made many seekers enlightened.

It has to be remembered that a man of the quality of Kakusan I call a religious man. Only one who knows his life can know his death; they are two sides of the same coin. If you have never known life, you will never know death. And to miss life and death and the whole beauty of both is to miss the very meaning of existence.

The sutra:

Beloved Buddha,
Once Kakusan went to see Kyōzan. Raising his foot, Kakusan said, "The twenty-eight Indian Patriarchs were like this" –
standing on one foot....

The meaning of it is: utter balance, no trembling inside, utter silence.

I am reminded of one of the most important disciples of Gautam Buddha, Vimalkirti. He was a great philosopher. When for the first time he came to see Buddha, he was very proud of his philosophical trainings. He said to Buddha, "You talk so much about freedom. What is freedom?"

Buddha said to Vimalkirti, "You can lift up one of your feet and stand on the other." He lifted his left foot up and was standing on the right foot when Buddha said, "Now, lift the right foot up also."

Vimalkirti said, "What nonsense! One foot is enough, two feet is impossible."

Buddha said, "You seem to be a man of understanding."

Freedom is standing on one foot; the other foot is responsibility. Freedom brings tremendous responsibility – not in the old sense that you have been told about, not as a duty, but as a spontaneous and conscious "response-ability."

There are two kinds of possibilities: either you react or you respond. A man who lives in his mind, reacts. He reacts according to his conditioning as a Christian, as a Hindu, as a Mohammedan. But his reaction is mechanical, any robot can do it. He has been conditioned to do it, hence he is doing it. But it is not out of his own spontaneity, it is not coming from his state of no-mind. When you respond from the state of no-mind – out of your meditation, not out of your conditioning – it is response, it is not reaction.

Freedom brings responsibility. You act not according to any commandments, you act not according to Manu or Moses or Jesus, you act according to your own light. And whenever you act according to your own light, there is immense fulfillment, a deep rejoicing.

> *Once Kakusan went to see Kyōzan. Raising his foot, Kakusan said, "The twenty-eight Indian Patriarchs were like this"* – standing on one foot in utter balance – *"and the six Patriarchs of the Country of T'ang were like this too, and you are like this, and I am like this!"*

Every man of consciousness has a tremendous balance in his life, in his actions, in his gestures. His whole life becomes a dance in balance. And those are the few people who have known the ultimate flowering of consciousness.

> *Kyōzan came down from the Zen seat and hit him four times with the wisteria staff.*

Kakusan was standing on one foot. *Kyōzan came down from the Zen seat and hit him four times with the wisteria staff* – the Zen staff. What is the meaning of this? He hit him four times because unless you can remain balanced in times of difficulties, in dark nights of the soul when the dawn seems to be almost impossible...when you have lost every hope of finding the truth, when you have lost the friend who was sharing his insight with you and you feel utterly blind, in all these situations if you can still remain balanced, then there is no problem. Your balance will start flowering on its own accord.

Hitting him four times, Kyōzan watched. Kakusan did not move, did not lose his balance, did not even ask him, "Why are you hitting me?" A man of balance does not care whether the night is dark, whether life is coming to an end. In every situation and circumstance his balance is never lost.

After Kakusan became enlightened, an ascetic once said to him, "What is the true meaning of Buddhism?" Kakusan remained silent and bowed to him.

Without saying a word, he has said more than can be said. His silence is not a dead, negative state. His silence is full of peace and love. He showed in his silence the meaning of the whole teaching of Buddha and to this stranger he bowed. It does not matter whether you are enlightened or not. In any case, in the deepest center of your being you are a buddha. And this is the very meaning of Buddha's whole teaching.

The ascetic asked, "Are you bowing to a man of the world?" Kakusan replied, "Don't you see what I am saying? I am your famous disciple!"

The man was an ordinary man of the world. He could not believe that an enlightened man, a buddha, would bow down to him. He was surprised. He said, "Don't you see, I am an ordinary man of the world. Are you bowing to a man of the world?"

Kakusan replied – what a beautiful answer – *"Don't you see what I am saying?"* And he has not said anything. But silence is also saying something. Bowing down is also saying something. *"Don't you see what I am saying? I am your famous disciple!"*

A man who is enlightened is the disciple of everyone in the world because what you cannot see, he can see with absolute clarity and certainty. Where you can see only a seed, he can see roses blossoming. Where you can at the most feel some potential, he sees your ultimate destiny. Where you are on the path, he sees you have reached home.

One of the most beautiful sayings that I have loved comes from Mahavira, a contemporary of Gautam Buddha. A very strange statement – Mahavira says, "If you have started the journey you have reached already."

If a seed has started sprouting the spring is not far away. Soon, where there was nothing there will be beautiful flowers, with great fragrance. Mahavira is saying that if you have started the journey you have already reached. You may not see it like that because your comprehension is very limited. You cannot see your own future flowering. But if a man of enlightenment cannot see either, then what is the difference? You are both blind.

> *At another time Kyōzan, on seeing a monk approach him, raised his mosquito flapper. At this, the monk shouted loudly, "Kwatz!"*
> *Kyōzan commented, "There is such a thing as saying 'Kwatz,' but tell me, where was my mistake?"*
> *The monk replied, "In improperly pointing to an external object" – at which Kyōzan hit him.*

A man like Kyōzan always points inwards. Whatever he does, whatever he says, is always pointing towards the internal.

Just on the margin... Gautam the Buddha never went outside the state of Bihar, except once. For forty-two years he went round and round in a small state. It has got its name, Bihar, because of Gautam Buddha's walking continuously around and around. 'Bihar' means the place where the Buddha walked.

He went only once out of Bihar, to Sarnath – a small village near Varanasi. But he stayed there only one day, and for twenty-five centuries people have been wondering.... He stayed in Vaishali at least twenty times, and in some places for many months because every rainy month he would not move; so every year for four months he stayed in one place. It's significant to note why he escaped from Sarnath after only one day.

There exists now in Sarnath a great institution teaching the philosophy of Buddha and his language, Pali. The director of the institute, Bhikkshu Jagdish Kashyap, invited me to his institute to speak on Gautam the Buddha, but I had to leave after one day. He had come to take me to the station. He said, "This is strange; why are you leaving after one day?"

I said, "For the same reason that Gautam Buddha left this place after one day."

He said, "It is strange, but we have been discussing..." and he was a Buddhist, "We have been discussing for all these centuries why he did not stay."

I said, "You are all idiots! Just see! I have moved around the whole country but I have never seen such big mosquitoes." And Buddha was not using mosquito nets. It would have been difficult carrying a mosquito net, he was traveling and traveling.

But I told Jagdish Kashyap, "You should at least give mosquito nets to every student and scholar and researcher in your institute, not only for the night but for the day too."

I stayed there for twenty-four hours inside a mosquito net!

Bashō wrote:

*Dying cricket
– how full of life,
his song.*

It is dying.... *Dying cricket – how full of life, his song.*

DYING CRICKET
– HOW FULL OF LIFE,
HIS SONG.

That is the way for the awakened one to live, with overflowing life, radiating with an abundance of energy; and that is the way for the awakened one to die, still radiating and overflowing his joy, his bliss, his ecstasy.

Maneesha has asked a question:

Beloved Buddha,
Did Gautama's consciousness enter You at Your conception or is it that over the years his consciousness has gradually become suffused with You? Is it true that Krishnamurti was a candidate for the Maitreya, but missed?

Maneesha, it is true that J. Krishnamurti was prepared by a great theosophical movement in every possible way to become a vehicle of Gautam Buddha. Certainly a few of the theosophical movement were aware of the wandering soul of the Buddha, and the time was ripe. But they forgot one thing: that you cannot prepare, condition, educate somebody to receive the consciousness of Buddha. Twenty-five years of torture, of all kinds of disciplines, reciting of scriptures…and when Krishnamurti was twenty-five, they thought, "Now he is ready. He knows the scriptures, he lives according to the precepts."

They did not allow him to join a public school, because others may contaminate his consciousness. They did not allow him to move in society, or to move around and meet anyone he wanted. Just a chosen group of the theosophical movement was surrounding him.

He was caught by them when he was only nine years of age. And from then on he had to get up at three o'clock in the morning, have a bath in the nearby river in Adyar, Madras, and then recite the Buddhist sutras. What a torture, you can imagine! And he was not at all interested; it was not his choice, it was circumstantial.

His mother died; his father, who was a poor clerk in the post office, had two sons and it was difficult for him to take care of them. And when Annie Besant, a famous lady, the president of the Theosophical Society, asked the father, he was immensely happy to get rid of them. Giving those two sons, Krishnamurti and Nityananda, he thought he was fulfilling his responsibility as a father. He could not manage it, but "these people have a worldwide movement; they will give them the best teaching that is possible."

It was under these circumstances, because the father was not able to take care of them, and the mother had died ...sometimes there was food, sometimes there was no food. Krishnamurti and Nityananda accepted, not knowing what was going to happen. And then started the long torture of discipline, of obedience, of surrender – because their understanding was: if Krishnamurti is perfectly ready intellectually and surrenders, the soul of Gautam Buddha will enter in him. That was their wrong conception.

After twenty-five years they declared the day, and six thousand theosophists from all over the world gathered in Holland, where the head office was. For Krishnamurti they had created a new branch of the theosophical movement, especially devoted to the world teacher that he was going to become by receiving the soul of Gautam Buddha. The organization was called "The Star of the East."

At a particular date, Krishnamurti was brought before six thousand delegates from all over the world. But on the stage he could see both things clearly: that he had no inclination at all, he had been forced – and whenever you force somebody, deep down there is a resentment – and this was the last moment to say the truth; after this there would be greater difficulties.

He refused to surrender, and he told the gathering, "I am not going to be the vehicle of Maitreya Buddha."

It was very shattering. The whole theosophical movement withered away. But Krishnamurti's failure is really the failure of imposed conditioning.

I am not in any way prepared by anybody. I have lived according to my light.

Maneesha, I had no reason to reject, because I have never been forced to do anything. It was a tremendously joyful moment to receive the greatest flowering of consciousness into my garden of being.

This does not make any change in me. This simply makes my silence richer, my words more true. I am not alone; now Gautam Buddha is also flying with me, together.

It is simply a meeting of two rivers. Neither one was under any compulsion.

J. Krishnamurti missed simply because he was overburdened by discipline. Otherwise, he was in every possible way capable. If he had grown the way I have grown – independently – he might have welcomed Maitreya. But unfortunately it was not to happen.

To remind you again, just to keep the distinction, Gautam the Buddha means the ancient Buddha. And according to his desire I will be known as Maitreya The Buddha.

Anando has brought a difficulty. All of you have now

become so accustomed to calling me Bhagwan. When she comes loaded with her secretarial work, without remembering she starts, "Hello, Bhagwan!" And then she repents: "I had been preparing all the way not to use this word 'Bhagwan', but the moment I saw you I forgot everything."

I have to help Anando and others also.

Buddha was called by his lovers, "Bhante" – which is far more refined, of greater implications. 'Bhante' means a friend who has gone far ahead – you are also on the path, but somebody is ahead of you.

So just to help you drop that old, ugly word 'Bhagwan', I suggest you use the word 'Bhante', at least for the transitory period. And if Anando does not come tomorrow with, "Hello, Bhante!" then the German Zen master, Niskriya, has to hit her three times with great compassion and love.

I will have to ask forgiveness from Sardar Gurudayal Singh. For a few days at least, many problems will be coming. They have to be sorted out, and I can ask only Gurudayal Singh.

Nivedano…

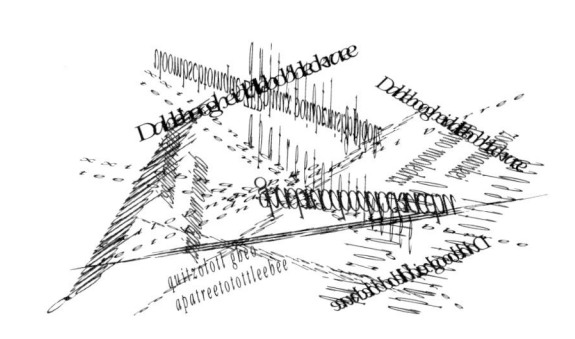

Nivedano...

> Be silent. Close your eyes. Feel your body to be completely frozen.
> Now this is the moment. Look inwards with the totality of your consciousness, with an urgency as if this is going to be the last moment of your life. Go like a spear, piercing into the very center of your being, deeper and deeper. The deeper you go, the closer you come to yourself. And to be close to yourself is to be the buddha.
>
> This moment is so blessed in that ten thousand consciousnesses are approaching closer and closer to the highest peak, the buddha.
> Remember, the word 'buddha' consists of only one quality: the witnessing.
> Witness – your body is not you.
> Witness – your mind is not you.
> Witness – that except witnessing you are no more.
>
> To make it clear,

Nivedano...

> Relax, but go on keeping the witnessing eye.
> At this moment you have made this evening a splendor, a living miracle. I can see the Buddha

Auditorium has become a lake of consciousness. All boundaries are dropped, you have melted just like ice into the oceanic. The auditorium has become a lake of consciousness without ripples. Thousands of flowers will start showering on you.

Remember to collect as much majesty, as much splendor as you can. And don't forget to persuade the buddha to come along with you, to fill your whole life, your smallest actions and words, gestures and silences.

Nivedano...

Come back, but come back utterly different, with grace, with silence, as a buddha. Just sit for a few moments remembering the golden path you have traveled, the eternal that you have experienced for a few moments at the center of your being, and a glimpse of the buddha that you have caught.

Slowly slowly persuade, go on persuading...
I know on my own authority if you persuade honestly, the buddha has to come and cover your whole life with joy, with immense beauty, and with a truth that brings liberation, freedom and immortality.

Okay, Maneesha?
Yes, Bhante.

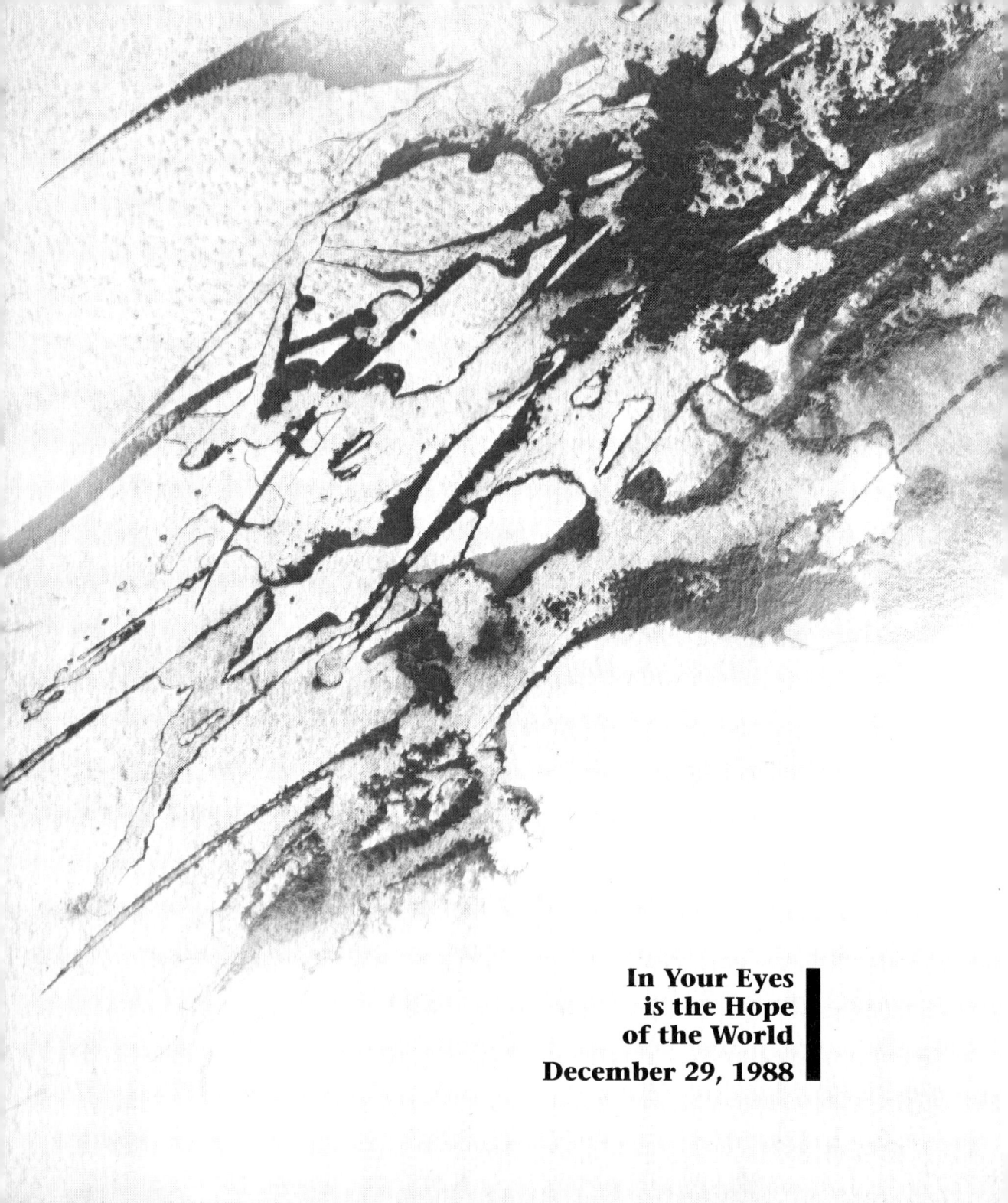

**In Your Eyes
is the Hope
of the World
December 29, 1988**

Beloved Buddha,

One day when Isan and the monks were engaged in picking tea leaves, Isan called to Kyōzan, "All day I have heard your voice and not seen you." Kyōzan, instead of saying anything, shook a tea plant.
Isan said, "You have got the use, but not the subject."
"I ask you, what do you say?" said Kyōzan. Isan kept silent.
Then Kyōzan said, "You have got the subject, but not the use."
More than ten disciples of Kyōzan's became enlightened.

A few years before Kyōzan passed away, he composed the following gatha:
   When my years reach
   seventy-seven
   my departure will take place.
   I will leave it to my nature
   to float or sink
   when I leave with my two hands
   embracing my folded knees.
At his death on Tung Ping mountain, in 890, he was seventy-seven years old and actually held his folded knees with both hands. The emperor bestowed upon him the posthumous title "Great Master Chih Tung" (meaning Wisdom Pervasion) and for his stupa the epigraph Miao Kuang (meaning Wonderful Light).

Maneesha, this time has been of historical importance.

For seven weeks I was fighting with the poison day and night. One night, even my physician, Amrito, became suspicious that perhaps I cannot survive. He was taking my pulse rate and heartbeats on his cardiogram. Seven times I missed one heartbeat.

The seventh time I missed a heartbeat, it was natural for his scientific mind to think, "Now we are fighting a battle that is almost lost." But I said to him, "Don't be worried. Your cardiogram can go wrong; it is just a mechanical device. Trust in my witnessing. Don't bother about my heartbeats."

On the last day of the seven weeks' struggle when all the pain from my body disappeared, Amrito could not believe it. It was happening almost like a miracle. Where has all the pain disappeared?

That last night, in the middle of the night I heard somebody knocking on the door. It is rare; nobody knocks on my door. I had to open my eyes. There was absolute darkness in the room, but I saw suddenly, with the door closed, a human being made of pure light entering. For a moment there was silence, and I heard from nowhere, "Can I come in?" The guest was so pure, so fragrant. I had simply to take him into the silences of my heart.

This body of pure light was nobody but Gautam the Buddha.

You can still see in my eyes the flame that I have absorbed into myself, a flame that has been for twenty-five centuries wandering around the earth to find a shelter. I am immensely blessed that Gautam the Buddha knocked on my doors.

You can see in my eyes the flame, the fire. Your inner being is made of the same cool fire. You have to carry this fire around the earth, sharing, from eyes to eyes, from heart to heart.

We are not here to create a new religion; our every effort is to destroy all religions. They have done enough harm to humanity. To tolerate them even for a single day is against anybody who understands the meaning of compassion, who understands the eternity of his own being. Unless all these organized religions become memories of the past, man cannot live without fetters, without chains, without moralities imposed on him against his will. He cannot live as an individual, he has to subdue himself according to the masses. That is the ugliest slavery.

But for thousands of years man has lived in slavery of many kinds. He has forgotten the taste of freedom. He has forgotten the beauty of responsibility. He has forgotten that he has wings, that the whole sky is his. And he need not be tied to a post like an animal, he is a bird of the beyond.

I will be continuing to create so much fire in you that it will burn your ego and your slavery simultaneously and make you a freedom, a light unto yourself. In your very eyes is the hope of the world.

But remember, even great symbols have been misunderstood.

Zarathustra was talking about this same fire, but his people have carried fire, ordinary fire, from Persia to India, persecuted by the Mohammedans. For centuries they have been keeping the same fire alive, which is simply absurd. That fire is not going to transform you, and Zarathustra did not mean that fire. I know Zarathustra just as I know myself.

Man has always been misunderstanding great symbols. And the men who have attained to the ultimate are helpless, they have to use symbols. Now I am saying, "the fire of my eyes." Don't repeat the same mistake as the people of Zarathustra have done.

Their temples are called *agiyari,* fire temples. For centuries they have carried the same fire; they don't allow it to go out, they go on refueling it. And not even for a single moment do they think: "What has this fire done for us? Certainly this is not the fire that Zarathustra was talking about."

Man is so blind, it is almost certain that he will misunderstand. He is not only blind, he is greedy.

When I came back from America, Govind Siddharth, one of my very old sannyasins told me, "You used to come to Ahmedabad, and just for you I have been keeping my ancestral home, because nobody lives there." His mother has died, his father has died, and one brother has gone to America. And Govind Siddharth lives in Bombay, has his business there.

He was certainly keeping a beautiful house. But when I told him, "I am no more going to move around the country; now whosoever is thirsty has to come to the well," he said, "I will sell the house."

He sold the house, and he informed me that, "Thirty-three lakh rupees are in the bank for your work whenever you want. Whatever the work, that money is there."

I asked him, "Is there any involvement with the family? Have you settled with your brother?"

He said to me, "Yes, the money is absolutely free now, just for your work."

After three days I told Neelam, who was working from Bombay as my secretary, to ask Govind Siddharth to transfer the money to one of the trusts, because I was going to move to Poona and tremendous forces were going to gather there. In three days his greed took over his great desire to work for me. He said, "Thirty-three lakhs is too much. I can only afford three lakhs."

Neelam told me that in just three days he has reduced it from thirty-three lakhs to three lakhs. I said, "Don't be worried. Just go and get the three lakhs." And when she reached him Govind Siddharth said, "It is very difficult. My whole family is involved in it" – I had asked him that before, and he had denied it. And I know for sure that the money has nothing to do with his family.

Neelam was shocked. She came running to me and said, "It is unbelievable that a man can turn about like this." I said, "Forget about that. You have another account of three lakh rupees, which has been donated from simple and loving people from all over the country. It is in your name and Govind Siddharth's name. It is not his money; please just take that money out of his hands."

She said, "Do you think he will change his mind about *that* money also, which is not his?" I said, "Man's blindness, his unconscious greed is vast enough. You just go, and be quick!"

And Govind Siddharth started playing games, saying, "I cannot allow you to take all of the three lakhs, because while

Bhagwan was not here I gave thirty-five thousand rupees for his work to the Bombay center. I will have to deduct that much money."

I told Neelam, "Let him deduct it, if thirty-five thousand can satisfy him" – which was not his money! Then too, it took almost one month to get the money out, leaving behind the thirty-five thousand without any reason except that his signature was needed. This money was paid for his signature.

And now I don't see him here. Perhaps he is afraid to look into my eyes, straight. I will not ask him about the money. I have never asked anybody about money, but I will for certain, absolutely for certain, look straight into his eyes. What kind of greed…!

And it is not that he has not loved me, but an unconscious love is a blind love. It is only a superficial hypocrisy, of which you are not aware.

Whatever I am imparting to you, please don't do the same as has been done down the ages by millions of people, misunderstanding or trying to manipulate things according to their own vested interest.

These sutras I am telling you just to remind you that if other people, simple and ordinary, were capable of becoming buddhas, it will be a shame if you die before you become a buddha. Let us make a deep commitment – not to anybody, but to yourself – that you are going to invest every breath for the ultimate purpose of being an eternal light, a lotus in full bloom. Without being a buddha you don't have any meaning in your life.

Maneesha has brought this anecdote:

Beloved Buddha,
One day when Isan and the monks were engaged in picking tea leaves, Isan called to Kyōzan – Isan was the master of Kyōzan – "All day I have heard your voice and not seen you." Kyōzan, instead of saying anything, shook a tea plant.

A beautiful gesture. He said, "You have been hearing the breeze passing through the tea plants. Of course, you could not see me, but you have heard, through the breeze passing through the tea plants, my voice."

Isan said, "You have got the use, but not the subject."

It is a very complicated statement.
He is saying, "You know how to use yourself, but you don't know who you are. You know the use but you don't know the subject. You have been cutting tea leaves perfectly well, but you were not aware. Where has your subjectivity been? Where has your witness been?"

"I ask you, what do you say?" said Kyōzan. Isan kept silent.
Then Kyōzan said, "You have got the subject, but not the use."

Being silent, I know you have entered into your innermost being, your subjectivity, but just being silent is not enough. Your silence must become a song. Your experience of enlightenment must come to enlighten all your activities.
"You have the subject, but not the use." Just being silent is not enough.

What a tremendous dialogue between the master and the disciple!

More than ten disciples of Kyōzan's became enlightened – listening to this dialogue.

Isan said, "You have the use but you don't have the subject." That was a partial statement. The remaining part is when Isan became silent and Kyōzan said, "You have got the subject but not the use."

Listening to this small dialogue of immense implications... What Isan and Kyōzan are discussing is how to bring the inner to the outer, how to bring the center to the circumference. How to bring your inner being into the marketplace, how to share it with your friends, with the strangers who are ready to share. Just listening to this small dialogue *more than ten disciples of Kyōzan's became enlightened.*

Enlightenment is not a process; it is an event. It is not something that takes years and years then finally you reach the goal. It is possible it may take years and years because you don't want to be enlightened right now. You may go round and round avoiding enlightenment – that takes time.

ENLIGHTENMENT

Otherwise, this very moment you are the buddha. Just a simple opening, a straight insight into your own being, and enlightenment happens suddenly. It is not a time phenomenon.

A few years before Kyōzan passed away, he composed the following gatha...

A few years before he passed away, he predicted in every minute detail how he is going to pass away.

*When my years reach
seventy-seven
my departure will take place.
I will leave it to my nature
to float or sink
when I leave with my two hands
embracing my folded knees.
At his death on Tung Ping mountain, in 890, he was* exactly seventy-seven years old and actually held his folded knees with both hands. The emperor bestowed upon him the posthumous title "Great Master Chih Tung" (meaning Wisdom Pervasion). And for his stupa, *for his memorial, the epigraph* – given by the emperor himself – was *Miao Kuang (Wonderful Light).*

That wonderful light brings me back....
You are full of wonderful light. You are made of it! But you wander around the world.

The world is vast and life is short. Don't waste your time wandering around the world for small positions, for gathering some money, some power. All that is just like writing on the sand. A small wind or just a wave coming in from the ocean and all the writing disappears.

Whatever you do outside yourself is nothing but writing on the sand, while a wonderful light waits within you – a light that has no source, a light that is not dependent on any fuel, a light that has been within you since eternity, a light that is your immortality. Just enter into yourself and you have entered the holiest temple of existence.

COMING
FROM NOWHERE,
DEPARTING
FOR NOWHERE,
A FLASHING GLANCE...
ENTERING
THE MYSTERY!

The death poem of Hsu-t'ang, who provided much inspiration for Ikkyu:

*Coming from nowhere,
Departing for nowhere,
A flashing glance...
Entering the mystery!*

Maneesha has asked a question.

*Beloved Buddha,
Is it not a paradox that You – who must be the most truly individualistic of beings – have proved also to be the purest medium for another?*

Maneesha, I am not the medium for anyone. Gautam Buddha is just my guest. It does not in any way interfere with my individuality. He knows it, there is no need to say it. He is not the man to interfere. He himself is one of the greatest individualists. That's why meeting with him is almost like meeting with oneself.

I am not anybody's medium. I have just found another companion, a tremendous force to help you. Now the caravan is not only to depend on my insights. Now my insights will also be supported by the greatest human being, Gautam Buddha.

And his choice to be my guest is simply because what he has known I have known, what he has become I have become. There is such a deep synchronicity that it is only in language I can say there is a division between the host and the guest. But in existential terms, the host and guest have become one. When two unbounded souls meet, it is a merger. It is just a merger like a river descending deep into the ocean and disappearing.

...Tonight, I will not take away Sardar Gurudayal Singh's time. He was kind enough yesterday.

Father Finger meets his arch-enemy, Rabbi Horowitz, on the street.

"Last night," says Father Finger, "I dreamt that I was in Jewish heaven. Man, Jewish heaven was a mess! Everybody was yelling and screaming, and eating, and waving their arms in the air; people were fighting about money – all kinds of chaos, and the noise was deafening."

"Well," replies Rabbi Horowitz, "that's strange. Last night I had a dream that I went to Christian heaven, but it was very different. Beautiful flowers everywhere, beautiful architecture, wide open streets, such peace and quiet all around."

"And the people?" asks Father Finger proudly.

"People?" answers the rabbi. "What people?"

It is another day at the elementary school and Mr. Smell, the teacher, is giving the class a test before he lets them go home.

"Now, Albert," says Smell, "can you give me the names of three fruits?"

"No," says Albert, looking out of the window. "I don't eat fruit."

"Okay, smart-ass," snaps Smell, "for that you can stay after class and do extra homework."

But after class, Smell calls Albert over and makes a deal with him. "Listen, Albert," he says, "if you take this letter to your sister, Ruby, I will let you go home, and you can tell me the three fruits tomorrow."

"Okay," shrugs Albert, taking the letter. But on his way home, he sneaks a look inside the letter and it reads: "Ruby, meet me at five o'clock behind the church."

So Albert delivers the letter to Ruby, his sister, and then at five o'clock he waits behind the church, and watches the secret meeting.

The next day in school Mr. Smell asks, "Okay, Albert, can you recite a sentence with three fruits in it?"

"Sure," says Albert. "If I catch you one more time putting your fat *banana* into my sister's *peach,* I'm going to kick you in your little pink *plums!*"

Gilbert Gurgle, who is seventy years old, is getting married for the sixth time. As he waits at the church door for the wedding to begin, he thinks of all the music played at his previous marriages.

The first time, he had been twenty years old. The band played: "There'll Be A Hot Time In The Old Town Tonight!"

When he got married the second time, at the age of thirty, it was to the tune: "If You've Got The Money, Honey, I've Got The Time."

At forty, they played the song: "Now and Then."

At fifty, it was: "I Don't Get Around Much Anymore."

When he reached sixty, marrying the fifth time, the music was: "The Thrill Is Gone."

His thoughts are interrupted as the church organ starts to play. Gilbert wobbles down the aisle to the tune of Michael Jackson's hit song: "Beat It!"

Now, Nivedano, beat it!   ((((•))))

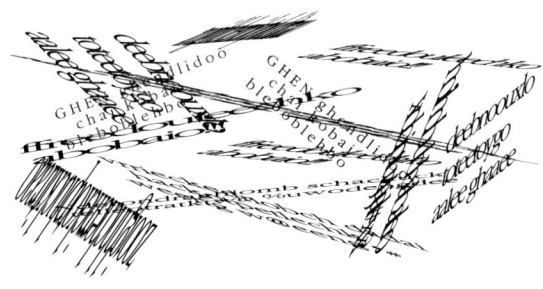

Nivedano...   ((((•))))

Be silent. Close your eyes. Feel your body to be completely frozen.

This is the moment to look inwards with your

total consciousness, and with an urgency as if this is the last moment of your life. Without such urgency and totality nobody has ever become enlightened. It is not a question of time, it is a question of deepening consciousness.

Deeper and deeper. Don't hold anything, because at the deepest center of your being you are going to encounter your real being, the buddha.

Just remember one thing: the only quality the buddha has is that of witnessing.

Remain centered and witness that you are not the body, you are not the mind, you are simply a witness.

To make it clear,

Nivedano...

Relax, and remember, remain centered in your witnessing.
It is here you will find the buddha.
It is here you will find the eternal fire.
It is here that your splendor is hidden.

The night was beautiful in itself, but the ten thousand buddhas melting into a lake of consciousness have made it majestic, a miracle.

There is no other miracle than becoming a buddha. The whole existence will rejoice with you. The trees will sing in their silence; the stars will dance in faraway skies, and invisible flowers will shower on you.

This moment is a historical moment. For centuries there has not been such a gathering.

Collect as many flowers and fragrances as possible, and persuade the buddha to come with you.

You have to be both – the subject and the use. Your buddha is not something to be worshipped; your buddha has to chop wood and carry water from the well. Your buddha has to become your very breathing, your very heartbeat – in all your actions the same grace, in your words the same poetry. Even your walking will become a dancing.

Nivedano...

Come back, but come back with great grace, with great beauty, with the silence of a buddha. Sit down for a few moments just to recollect the golden path you have been on, reaching to your very center.

And around the clock remember to remain a witness, and soon you will be filled with what I have been calling the buddha.

Okay, Maneesha?
Yes, Buddha.

I Am Just Myself
December 30, 1988

Beloved Buddha,

Chōsa was a disciple of Nansen and a contemporary of Tokusan, Rinzai and Isan. One day Chōsa went for a walk and when he returned to the gate, the head monk asked him, "Oshō, where have you been strolling?"

Chōsa replied, "I have come from walking in the hills."

The head monk said, "Where have you been?"

Chōsa said, "First I went following the fragrant grasses, and now I have returned in pursuit of the falling blossoms."

At this the head monk commented, "You are full of the spring."

Chōsa replied, "Better than the autumn dews falling on the lotus leaves."

One evening Chōsa (who was Kyōzan's "uncle" in the dharma lineage) was enjoying the moonlight with Kyōzan, who said, "Everyone has 'this one thing' but does not know how to use it."

Chōsa replied, "Perhaps I should employ you and use it."

Kyōzan exclaimed, "Try it!"

Instantly, Chōsa trampled on Kyōzan.

Kyōzan then commented, "Uncle, you are like a fierce tiger!"

My Beloved Ones,

These four days have been of immense difficulty to me. I had thought that Gautam Buddha would be understanding of the change of times, but it was impossible. I tried my hardest, but he is so much disciplined in his own way – twenty-five centuries back – he has become a hard bone.

Small things became difficult.

He used to sleep only on the right side. He did not use a pillow; he used his hand as a pillow. The pillow was, for him, a luxury.

I told him, "The poor pillow is not a luxury, and it is sheer torture to keep your hand the whole night under your head. And do you think to lie down on the right side is right, and the left is wrong? As far as I am concerned, this is my basic fundamental, that I synthesize both the sides."

He was eating only one time per day and he wanted, without saying a word, that I should do it also. He used to beg his food. He asked me, "Where is my begging bowl?"

This evening exactly at six o'clock when I was taking my jacuzzi, he became very much disturbed – "Jacuzzi?" Taking a bath twice a day was again a luxury.

I said, "You have fulfilled your prophecy that you will be coming back. Four days are enough – I say goodbye to you! And now you need not wander around the earth; you just disappear in the ultimate blue sky.

"You have seen for four days that I am doing the work that you wanted to do, and I am doing it according to the times and the needs. I am not in any way ready to be dictated to. I am a free individual. Out of my freedom and love I have received you as a guest, but don't try to become a host."

These four days I have been having a headache. I had not

known it for thirty years, I had completely forgotten what it means to have a headache. Everything was impossible. He is so accustomed to his way, and that way is no longer relevant.

So now I make a far greater historical statement, that I am just myself.

You can continue to call me The Buddha, but it has nothing to do with Gautam the Buddha or Maitreya the Buddha. I am a buddha in my own right. The word 'buddha' simply means the awakened one.

It will be a great difficulty for poor Anando, because now I declare that my name should be Shree Rajneesh Zorba The Buddha.

I have to offer an apology to Katue Ishida, the seeress in an ancient Shinto shrine in Japan. I tried my hardest to accommodate a twenty-five centuries old, out-of-date individuality, but I am not ready to be in a self torture.

And Anando has to see me afterwards, to release the second story... because that makes me absolutely free from any kind of tradition. I used to think that Gautam Buddha is an individual – and that is true, he is. But even against his desire a tradition has arisen in Tibet, in China, in Japan, in Sri Lanka, and I don't want to struggle with these idiots. I want to work with my own people on my own authority.

Maneesha has asked:

Beloved Buddha,
Chōsa was a disciple of Nansen and a contemporary of Tokusan, Rinzai and Isan.
One day Chōsa went for a walk and when he returned to the gate, the head monk asked him, "Oshō, where have you been strolling?"
Chōsa replied, "I have come from walking in the hills."
The head monk said, "Where have you been?"
Chōsa said, "First I went following the fragrant grasses, and now I have returned in pursuit of the falling blossoms."
At this the head monk commented,
"You are full of the spring."
Chōsa replied,
"Better than the autumn dews falling on the lotus leaves."

One evening Chōsa (who was Kyōzan's "uncle" in the dharma lineage) was enjoying the moonlight with Kyōzan, who said, "Everyone has 'this one thing' but does not know how to use it."
Chōsa replied, "Perhaps I should employ you and use it."
Kyōzan exclaimed, "Try it!"
Instantly, Chōsa trampled on Kyōzan.
Kyōzan then commented, "Uncle, you are like a fierce tiger!"

A small but very beautiful anecdote.

Zen always tries to beautify the ordinary; it gives greater meanings and implications to words of the ordinary world.

So you have to remember that these statements not only say what you hear, but they say much which you can hear only in your silences.

Chōsa had been strolling in the hills. When he returned, the head monk said, "Where have you been?"

Chōsa said, "First I went following the fragrant grasses..."

This is a way of saying that "First I was following only the very ordinary grasses and their fragrance – I thought this was immensely beautiful – *and now I have returned in pursuit of the falling blossoms."*

The difference between the fragrant grasses and the falling blossoms is the same as the difference between you unaware, and you utterly full of light and awareness.

The distinction between the grasses and the blossoms is the same as between you *not knowing* that you are a buddha, and the moment you know that you *are* a buddha. You have always been a buddha. In fact, there is no way to be otherwise.

Buddha is completely blossomed, fully opened. His lotuses, his petals, have come to a completion, a perfection beyond which it is difficult, almost impossible, to go.

*At this the head monk commented,
"You are full of the spring."*

A man of silence, a man who has been following the falling blossoms, also becomes part of the spring – the beautiful time when exotic flowers blossom with the fragrances of the beyond. Certainly he was full of spring.

Every day you experience it. Every day you become full of spring. I am trying my best to use the words only to indicate to you the path that is beyond the words. Whenever you are at the center of your being, blossoms start falling and you are full of spring – and a spring that has no beginning and no end.

Chōsa replied, "Better than the autumn dews falling on the lotus leaves."

Certainly, to be full of spring yourself is far more beautiful than the autumn dews falling on the lotus leaves. That is one of the most beautiful things to watch: when autumn dews fall on the lotus leaves and shine in the morning sun like real pearls.

But of course it is a momentary experience. As the sun rises, the autumn dews start evaporating. Soon there will be no autumn dews. A few will have evaporated into the air, a few will have slipped down from the leaves, to the ocean, but all will be gone within a few minutes.

This temporary beauty cannot be compared, certainly, with an eternal spring in your being. You look back as far as you

I AM JUST MYSELF

can, and it has always been there. You look forward as much as you can, and you will be surprised: it is your very being. Wherever you are it will be there, and the flowers will continue to shower on you. This is spiritual spring.

> *One evening Chōsa (who was Kyōzan's "uncle" in the dharma lineage) was enjoying the moonlight with Kyōzan, who said, "Everyone has 'this one thing'...."*

What is this one thing that Kyōzan mentioned? This one thing is your consciousness. Nothing can be said about it, because it is as invisible as the air. Nothing can be done to it, because it is born perfect.

> Chōsa's comment was,
> *"Perhaps I should employ you and use it."*
> *Kyōzan said, "Try it!"*
> *Instantly, Chōsa trampled on Kyōzan.*

What can be the significance of Chōsa trampling upon Kyōzan?
He is saying, "This body that I am trampling, you are not. And this mind that is asking me to try it, you are not. But while I am trampling you, deep down I can see your witness. This witness is the one thing, the most important, the most significant – the only thing which is incomparable in the whole existence."

> *Kyōzan then commented, "Uncle, you are like a fierce tiger!"*

Obviously, he trampled on Kyōzan to make it clear to him

that "you are only the watcher." And that is the only thing which cannot be said, cannot be explained, but can only be indicated. And the way he indicated it is the way of a tiger or a lion.

Moritake wrote:

*A morning glory!
And so, today,
may seem my own life story.*

The morning glory is one of the most beautiful flowers – particularly in the Far East. And Moritake, an enlightened master, is saying:

"A morning glory...it opens itself as the sun rises, as the birds start singing, as the whole atmosphere becomes cool with the morning breeze. And the morning glory has a tremendous perfume."

*And so, today,
may seem my own life story.*

Moritake is saying, "The dark night of my soul has ended. The dawn that I have been searching for millions of lives has finally arrived. The sun is rising and the morning glory suddenly has opened and thrown its perfume to the breeze to take it as far away as possible.

"It seems to me," says Moritake, "this is my whole life story. My being has also come to a flowering, and in the very innermost core my sun has risen. The night is over and the day of my awakening has started. This day of awakening and awareness knows no end."

Gautama the Buddha is reported to have said, "The night has no beginning, it is eternal, and the morning has no end – it is also eternal. The night is the past that has gone away, and the morning is that which is coming slowly, settling, settling forever."

Maneesha has asked:

Beloved Buddha,
Since You became a host for Gautama the Buddha, You seem quite different to me, and meditating in Your physical presence is also different. It is not just the impact of seeing You again after an absence, because the feeling has not diminished with time; nor is it just my fantasy, because others feel the same way.
Your love seems a little less like a cuddle and more like a boiling cauldron.

Maneesha, you were right before six o'clock this evening. Now your question is irrelevant.
Okay?

Nivedano...

I AM JUST MYSELF

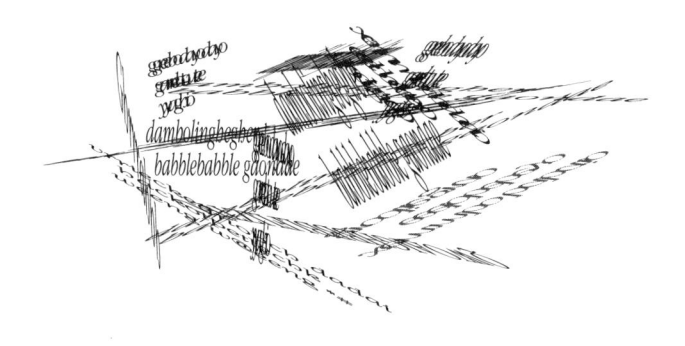

Nivedano...

Be silent. Close your eyes. Feel your body to be completely frozen.

Now, this is the moment to look inwards with your total consciousness, and with an urgency as if this is going to be your last moment in life.

Go deeper. As you will be reaching deeper and deeper and deeper, closer to your center, you will find the buddha – not any buddha of the past, but your very being.

Everybody is a born buddha, whether one remembers it or not. This is the moment to remember it! Because with the very remembrance of your being a buddha, a new world opens its doors.

Just be a witness.

Nivedano, make it clear...

Just watch the body – it is not you. This is the body which can be trampled. Watch the mind – it is not you. The only quality that you can claim as your very being is witnessing. And witnessing makes you a buddha.

Gather as much as you can the silences of your heart, and the tremendous peace that has descended over you. The whole spring – gather it! And persuade the buddha to come along with you, to become your very breathing, to become your ordinary life.

Sooner or later there will not be anyone here who is not a buddha in his own right. Before Nivedano calls you, persuade the buddha.

Today, it is not only to come and sit silently for a few minutes, but also to dance because I have declared myself Zorba The Buddha, which has been my basic approach to all human problems. This evening is far more significant than the evening four days before.

Come back. Bring all your silence and joy and grace with you. Sit a few moments utterly full of spring.

Today you have to stand up and dance with the music, because this is my last declaration.

Okay, Maneesha?
Yes, Buddha.

My Change Has Taken Me Higher
December 31, 1988

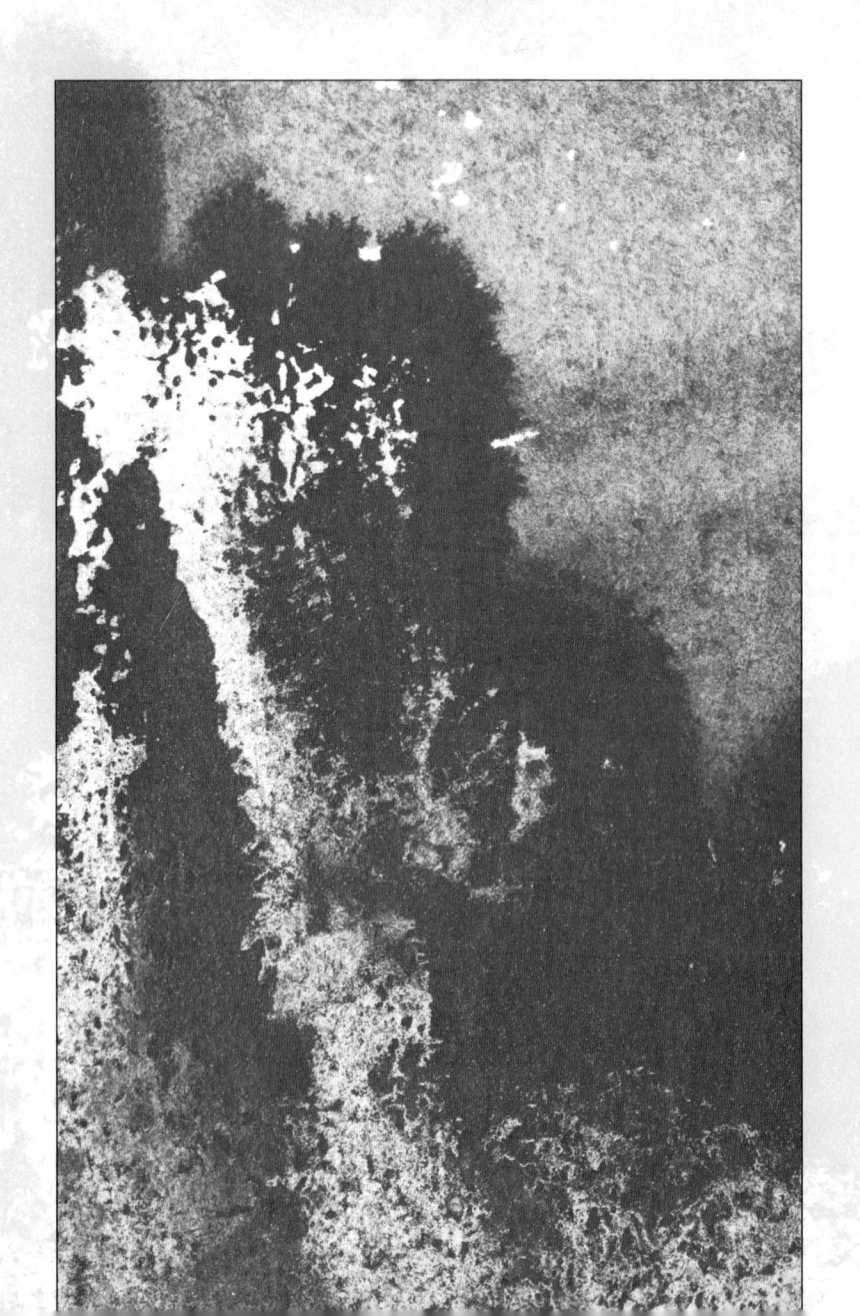

Beloved Buddha,

*Once a disciple of Ma Tzu, called Ikan,
was asked by a monk,
"Has the dog the buddha-nature or not?"
Ikan replied yes, and the monk then asked,
"Have you got it or not?"
Ikan responded, "I have not."
Then the monk asked,
"All existent creatures have the buddha-nature;
how is it that you haven't?"
Ikan said, "I don't belong to all existent creatures."
The monk commented,
"You say you don't belong to all existent creatures.
This 'You' – is it a buddha or not?"
Ikan said, "It is not a buddha."
The monk then inquired,
"What sort of thing, in the last resort, is this 'You'?"
Ikan replied, "It is not a thing."
The monk continued,
"Can it be perceived or thought of?" –
at which Ikan concluded,
"Thought cannot attain to it; it cannot be fathomed.
For this reason, it is said to be a mystery."*

My Beloved Ones,

Geeta had to inform Katue Ishida, the seeress and the prophetess of one of the most ancient shrines of the Shinto religion in Japan. Geeta was a little concerned that she would be disturbed and shocked, but on the contrary, Ishida was immensely happy.

She said, "I have not only prophesied that Gautam Buddha would be entering your master's being; I have also prophesied that, just as Buddha himself changed his name four times, your master would also do the same."

She said, "My only concern is your master's health and his work. It does not matter whether Buddha remains in his being or not."

I am immensely grateful to Ishida for understanding the situation with clarity.

Yes, it is true Gautam Buddha changed his name four times. And as I remember it, it was not worthy of him to do that. My change has taken me higher.

I found Buddha too old and too much fixed in his approach to life. Finally I dropped all concern with anyone. I have chosen my own name: Zorba the Buddha.

It has meaning, it is not just a name. It is my whole *philosia;* it is my whole vision, in which the lowest will meet with the highest, in which materialism and spiritualism will not be two separate and antagonistic things. That division has killed human spirit immensely. It has made man a battlefield, and I want man to be a dance, a harmony, a balance.

But Gautam Buddha's changing of names is a little unworthy of him.

I have no concern to protect anybody; now I am going to

be simply stating the truth. Whether it hurts, wounds, or heals, depends on you.

Gautam Buddha's name as given by his parents was Siddharth. It was a perfect name – the name of Buddha does not go higher than Siddharth. Siddharth means "one who has achieved the meaning of life." What more do you want?

Then, at that time there was a great competition which makes me laugh – a competition amongst Mahavira, Gautam Buddha and six others of the same category.

The Jaina lineage is perhaps the most ancient. In one *kalpa* – which means four million years – there will be only twenty-four Jaina *tirthankaras*. Twenty-three had already happened, only one last seat was vacant, and all these eight people were competing to be the twenty-fourth *jinna*. *Jinna* means "the conqueror of oneself."

Buddha was also in the competition. It makes me feel very ashamed. He wanted to change his name to Siddharth Jinna. Jinna means the conqueror, but he could not defeat Mahavira – not because he was less conscious, but because he was not such a great ascetic. Mahavir was almost a masochist; he disciplined his life along the lines of self-torture. And unfortunately, humanity is still sadistic; it wants people to torture themselves. Just

> *Now I am going to be simply stating the truth. Whether it hurts, wounds, or heals, depends on you.*

by self-torture they become respectable saints.

Buddha could not manage; neither could the six others, and Mahavira was appointed as the twenty-fourth and the last prophet of Jainism. Feeling defeated... In the first place to be competitive is not a right quality for a religious man. To be competitive is very ordinary and worldly. You have renounced the world – from where does this competition arise? You have not renounced your mind, you have not renounced your ego. This is an expression of ego, to be the last tirthankara of a very respectable lineage.

And then, when he was defeated, he was in utter despair. He changed his name from Siddharth. Instead of being called the Jinna, he chose another word, similar: the Buddha. Then things become even more complicated, because Mahavira had twenty-three predecessors, and that was hurting to Gautam Buddha's ego. He visualized twenty-three absolutely imaginary Buddhas who had preceded him.

Never in any scripture is there any mention of these Buddhas. Jaina tirthankaras are mentioned in Hindu scriptures too, not only in Jaina scriptures. But the twenty-three Buddhas imagined by Gautam Buddha – just to complete the score of twenty-four – shows that even the greatest minds fall many times before they come to the completion and stop falling.

Katue Ishida is neither Buddhist nor has she any connection with me. She seems to be a woman of immense understanding, love, and search for a man who has arrived home. She is poor, because she has lived along the lines of non-possessiveness. That's why she has been delayed; now she is collecting money to come here to pay her respects.

Geeta could not believe it. She was thinking that Ishida

would be disturbed that her prophecy did not come true, or failed on the way. But an authentic seeker is not concerned with individuals. She told Geeta, "Don't feel worried and concerned. With every change your master has reached a higher stage."

This series of talks I would like to be dedicated with love and blessings to Katue Ishida.

Just because of her prophecy about me she has suddenly become a world-famous name. Now the news media are approaching to her to ask about the prophecy – on what grounds, and all kinds of questions. She has lived silently in a shrine deep in the forest, but just a single prophecy has brought her into the light. She needs to be brought into the light, she may be helpful in solving many problems that man is encountering.

But man's way of encountering problems is always strange and blind. For example, just now one of the most organized Jaina sects, *Terapanth,* is bombarded – particularly the head of the sect, Acharya Tulsi – with exposures upon exposures, almost in a chain.

Two disciples of Acharya Tulsi left the fold and exposed all the perversion, the sexual exploitation in the name of religion. Acharya Tulsi has more than seventeen hundred monks and double that number of nuns. It is a vast community of monks and nuns, and the exposures from these two – and since then others have joined – reveal all kinds of perverted practices, homosexuality, heterosexuality, and the nuns are being treated almost like prostitutes. The monks are either heterosexual, exploiting the nuns, or many of them are homosexual. And they all have taken the vow of celibacy!

Acharya Tulsi tried, through the government, to have the

book banned. But the publisher was very insistent, and he was ready to go to the court against the government. Seeing the situation, that to be in the court would mean more exposures, more dirt, Acharya Tulsi stopped the action. The books have been released.

One of these monks, Satish Kumar, had come to me when he left Acharya Tulsi's camp, thinking that I have been always against Acharya Tulsi and his whole philosophy. But I told him, "It does not matter, I will not exploit the situation, because to me it is not a question of Acharya Tulsi. That's how for centuries we have been treating symptoms, and we never go deep to the roots."

Acharya Tulsi is not at fault. Neither are his monks and nuns at fault. The fault is centuries old – as long as celibacy has been preached there has been sexual perversion.

I would like Acharya Tulsi to gather courage and come into the open, rather than trying to hide. It is not his fault, it is the fault of the society that imposes on their monks and nuns unnatural things like celibacy.

I will support Acharya Tulsi. I am always ready for any unpopular challenge! But he has to gather courage. Of course he will lose his respect, but it is better to lose your respect than to lose the truth.

All these monks – Jaina or Hindu, Christian or or any other religion – have lived in deep hypocrisy down the ages, and they are afraid that if they say the truth they will lose their prestige. Nobody will respect their truth.

This is a strange society. Everybody talks about truth and respect for truth, but just try one truth, and immediately you will see how you are condemned and your truth is distorted.

But there are only two possibilities for Acharya Tulsi and

MY CHANGE HAS TAKEN ME HIGHER

his thousands of monks and nuns: either to remain in the ancient hypocrisy or to come out and declare clearly that "It is not our fault. It is the fault of the tradition, of the religion which has imposed on us something unnatural." And whenever there is something unnatural, perversion is bound to happen.

But strangely enough, everybody is against Acharya Tulsi but nobody is against celibacy. And the fault is in the idea of celibacy, not in Acharya Tulsi or some other shankaracharya or the pope. It does not matter who the person is; the problem is whether in some way your society helps him to be unnatural, respects him if he becomes unnatural. Then you are distorting his very being. And to gain respect, people are ready; to be saints, people are ready. But from the back door once in a while you will see these same saints in situations you cannot conceive.

The problem is, the saint tries to keep his respect – and the society that follows him also tries to hide all perversions, because if all the saints that they have worshipped are exposed, that will degrade their religion, their respectability also. So both the society, the organized religion, and the unnatural, perverted hypocrites are always joining together to protect an unnatural style of living.

It is good that Acharya Tulsi is exposed, but I don't think it is his fault. He was ordained when he was only fourteen years old. Now what does a fourteen-year-old understand about celibacy? All that he understands is that the whole society is respecting him, he is carried on their shoulders; his own elders are touching his feet. Not only has he become a hero, his family has also become holy with him.

Now converting a fourteen-year-old child – do you think

he will be able to remain unnatural his whole life? That will be such a torture and a nightmare. He will have to find some solution, in such a way that his respectability remains and everything that he does is being done in darkness. But once in a while somebody comes out and exposes it – has to.

Satish Kumar, when he came to see me in 1960, was a young man with tremendous fire, and he told me the story of what happened to him – all kinds of sexual perversion. He became so ugly in his own eyes. He said, "I had gone to seek truth there, and I am being used and abused in every possible way."

You will be surprised to know that the nuns are being used sexually, and when they become old, the acharya in Jainism has the power to order them to commit suicide. Of course it has a beautiful religious name, it is not called suicide. But just by changing names things don't change. It is called *santhara*, and santhara means dying by fasting – a slow kind of torturous death. When a woman becomes too old, and to carry her is now useless – she has been used utterly, she has no other purpose – she is ordered to commit suicide through fasting. And she has to follow the order of the acharya: disobedience is sin.

But this whole humanity seems to be so asleep that nobody wants to go to the roots. And things are absolutely clear: except with brain surgery you cannot be celibate, unless you are born impotent.

But do you understand? Has any impotent person contributed anything to the world down the ages? – a painting, a poetry, a song, a music, a dance? Is there any impotent person around the world in the whole history of man who has contributed anything?

In fact all creation is part of sexual energy. Sexual energy is nothing but the creative force. If it can generate new life, it can generate millions of things. All creative people are oversexual; only mediocre people have average sexuality. That's why great poets cannot remain with one woman, great painters cannot remain with one woman. They have so much sensitivity, so much perception, that once is enough. Twice is stupid.

But one thing is certain: that even if you cut off the genitals – which has been done; in Russia before the revolution there was a vast Christian sect which was cutting off the genitals. And the person who was cutting his genitals was received as a great saint. Poor women, finding nothing to cut, started cutting off their breasts, and they were also respected as great and holy.

But I want you to know that by cutting off the genitals you cannot destroy sexuality. It will become cerebral, it will move in your mind, because the real center of sexual energy is not in the genitals. The real center is in your brain. Stimulating that center, you can immediately feel your genitals being stimulated. Just imagine a beautiful woman…you are thinking in the head, and there is a wireless service!

Unless a man's mind is surgically operated upon, nobody can be celibate. But the moment you surgically operate the sexual center, the person will become absolutely useless, utterly lousy – you will put him up and he will sit back down! He has lost his life energy, he has no more spine.

But such… And there are many practices of the same category which have been promoted by all the religions all over the world. I condemn them all without any exception, categorically, with absolute authority!

Medical science should be consulted before you give

initiation into celibacy. Unfortunately, even our doctors are so impotent they won't speak the truth. They *know* it! Even our doctors I have seen going to touch the feet of a saint who is thought to be celibate. Doctors? One simply wants to cry!

These idiots have been carrying degrees from western universities; they know perfectly that celibacy is not possible. But their minds are so conditioned that through mantra, through yoga, through some device, some spiritual worship, prayer, perhaps celibacy is possible.

I want to challenge on this occasion the medical association of India to investigate the case of Tulsi and his followers. And that will be very definitive – because it will be the same with your shankaracharyas, your bishops and your popes.

> *All creative people are oversexual; only mediocre people have average sexuality.*

Once and for all it has to be decided that fighting with sex is self-destructive. Use the sexual energy in a multi-dimensional way. Everything is created by the same energy. It is not only for reproduction, it is also for the creation of music, painting, poetry.

Just because of celibacy two things have happened in all the religions: they have become uncreative, and they have all become perverted. And they are the people dominating the society: they *preach* to you and they do just the opposite, just the very contrary.

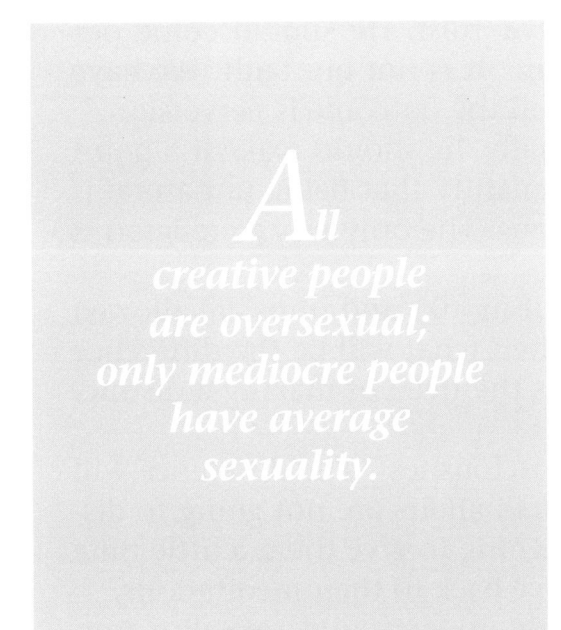

It is time! It is the end of the twentieth century, and your saints and your religions and your bishops and your priests are still living in primitive ages, barbarious. Then when somebody is exposed, the *person* is condemned, it is not that the roots are found.

I am absolutely with Acharya Tulsi. He should come out and expose the whole tradition: "It is not our fault. We have been forced to be unnatural, and the outcome is perversion."

Rather than taking it personally, he should make it a point to indicate to the whole of humanity that being unnatural is almost equal to being unreligious. The only way to religion is to be more and more natural.

You will be wondering that if monks and nuns are allowed to have sexual relationships, then what will be the difference between us and them? What is the need of making a distinction?

The difference will be of consciousness. The difference will be of meditation. And their small affairs are not going to distract their meditation, but are going to give them a little time to relax and play and then move back to their meditations.

Now, as the situation is, this underground sexuality running all over religious sects... They go on preaching against birth control methods, so they cannot use them and they cannot find anybody who is going to supply them. So many women, young women become pregnant, and the only way is in some way to commit suicide. Call it santhara, call it whatever you want, but I want to be direct and straightforward.

Maneesha has brought a beautiful anecdote:

Beloved Buddha,
Once, a disciple of Ma Tzu, called Ikan, was asked by a monk,

"Has the dog the buddha-nature or not?"
Ikan replied yes, and the monk then asked, "Have you got it or not?"

At first the monk was thinking that Ikan, a disciple of Ma Tzu, would hesitate a little in saying that a dog has a buddha-nature. But Ikan was almost coming to his spring. He said, "The dog has the buddha-nature, although hidden very deep. Perhaps it will take many many lives for the dog to discover it, but that does not matter. At the very center of the dog's being, the buddha is."

Ikan replied "Yes," and the monk was a little worried. He provoked him more; he said, "Okay, what about you? Do you have it or not?"

Ikan responded, "I have not."

It was a very strange answer, but of ultimate importance.

The monk asked, "All existent creatures have the buddha-nature; how is it that you have not?"
Even the dog has; you yourself said so.

Ikan said, "I don't belong to all existent creatures."
The monk commented, "You say you don't belong

to all existent creatures. This 'You' – is it a buddha or not?"
Ikan said, "It is not a buddha."
The monk then inquired,
"What sort of thing, in the last resort, is this 'You'?"
Ikan replied, "It is not a thing."
The monk continued, "Can it be perceived or thought of?" –
at which Ikan concluded,
"Thought cannot attain to it;
it can not be fathomed.
For this reason, it is said to be
a mystery."

When I say the 'buddha-nature' it is exactly equivalent to saying the mysterious nature, the ultimate mystery of existence.

Bashō wrote:

Spring too, very soon!
They are setting the scene for it –
plum tree and moon.

Preparing the ground, preparing the stage for the spring to come soon ...he is not talking about the outside spring; he is talking about the inside spring. That has also to be soon, but you should be preparing just like the plum tree and the moon are preparing for the outer spring. Except you, nobody can prepare the inner spring.

> SPRING TOO,
> VERY SOON!
> THEY ARE SETTING
> THE SCENE FOR IT –
> PLUM TREE
> AND MOON.

Maneesha has asked a question:

Apparently the "Akashic Daily Chronicle" newspaper ran an interview with Gautama. As a result, Krishna and Christ are packing their bags for their second coming – destination, Poona. Gautama told them that living with You was really something, and so they want to check out the scene for themselves.
Any comment?

Maneesha, please try to prevent them, because I have burned my fingers with Gautam Buddha – that's enough! No more disturbance in my sleep; no more knocking on my doors. These fellows are good from far away. To live in the same room or in the same body...those four days I will never forget!

After many many days, the time for Sardar Gurudayal Singh has come.

Father Fumble is thumbing through the church records one day, when he notices that one of his flock, Hamish McTavish, does not seem to have given any money to the church charities. The young priest decides to pay a call on Hamish, who is rumored to be very rich, and see if he can squeeze any money out of him.

"The records show," says Father Fumble, "that you have never donated any money to our charities."

"That's right," says Hamish. "And do your records also show that I have a crippled uncle who is completely unable to take care of himself? Furthermore," continues Hamish, "do they show that my sister was left a widow with ten children to take care of and no insurance or other means of support?"

"Well, no," says Father Fumble, a little embarrassed. "Our records do not show that."

"So," replies Hamish, "why should I give anything to *you*, when I don't give anything to *them?*"

Old Grandpa Babblebrain is finally persuaded to take his grandchildren, Biff and Bippy, to the zoo for the day. Biff and Bippy are really having a great time as they drag Grandpa here and there, pointing out the animals.

Grandpa is going a little senile, and is not always too sure where he is, or what he is doing. Then Bippy points into one cage and shouts, "Oh! Grandpa, look! That is a laughing hyena!"

Grandpa looks at the animal, and does not recognize it at all. "I don't believe it," says Grandpa. So he goes over to the zookeeper and asks what kind of animal it is.

"Yup," says the zookeeper, "it is a laughing hyena, alright."

"What is so special about this animal?" asks Grandpa.

"Well," says the zookeeper, "he only eats once a day."

"Hm," says Grandpa, "just like me."

"And," continues the zookeeper, "he only takes a bath once a week."

"Hm," says Grandpa, "just like me."

"And," says the zookeeper, "he only makes love once a year."

"Hm," says Grandpa, shaking his head. "Then why is he laughing?"

Chief Boonga, the head of a primitive African tribe, writes a letter to Pope the Polack at the Vatican. The Polack pope had sent three missionaries to the Boonga tribe a few months before.

"Your Holiness," writes Chief Boonga, "I would like to thank you personally for sending out the three Catholic missionaries to us. I and my tribe found them kind, compassionate, loving, wise, sensitive – and absolutely delicious!"

Nivedano...

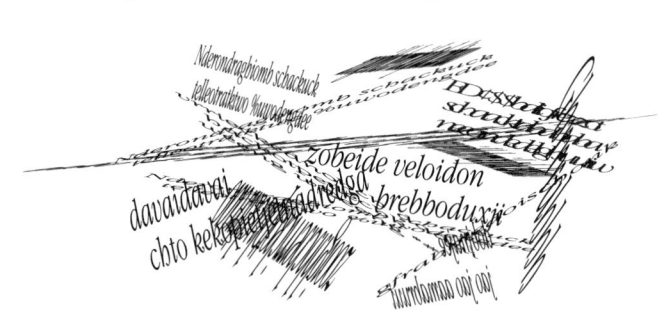

Nivedano...

Be silent. Close your eyes, and feel your body to be completely frozen.

This is the moment you can look inwards with your total consciousness, and with an urgency as if this is going to be your last moment. Only with such urgency can you reach to your very center *immediately!* And to be at your very center is to be a buddha. There is nothing beyond it.

In this silence, in this blissfulness, this night

becomes golden, something of the beyond.

Just remember one thing: the only quality of a buddha is to be a witness. The moment you are just a witness…looking at the body, you are not it; looking at the mind, you are not it. You are just the witness. Immediately you are transformed into a totally different world.

To make it clear, Nivedano…

Relax, but remember your witness. Whether you are sitting or lying or walking, your witness is always at the center, utterly still – just like a statue of a buddha. Flowers will start showering over you, the spring has come so suddenly. The Buddha Auditorium has become a lake of consciousness without any ripples.

Collect as much life energy, collect as many flowers as the spring breeze has brought within you. You have to bring them back and persuade the buddha to come along with you. It is your very nature. There is no question that it will not be persuaded; it has always been persuaded.

Unless the buddha becomes your very life – your walking, your working, your speaking, your silence – unless it becomes all that you are, you are not awakened. And without being awakened you miss life, its meaning, and you will miss your death and its meaning.

Only a buddha does not miss even a single drop

of existential beauty, blissfulness and ecstasy.

Nivedano...

Come back. But come back like a buddha – silently, peacefully, with a great grace. Sit just for a few minutes to remember and to recall the golden path you have traveled upon, the ultimate peace at the center of your being, and the experience of buddha nature, another name for the eternity of your being.

Inch by inch, buddha is coming closer to you. Just arrange the path for him. The spring is guaranteed to come; so is buddha.

Okay, Maneesha?
Yes, Buddha.

The World of the Gurus has Ended
January 1, 1989

Beloved Buddha,

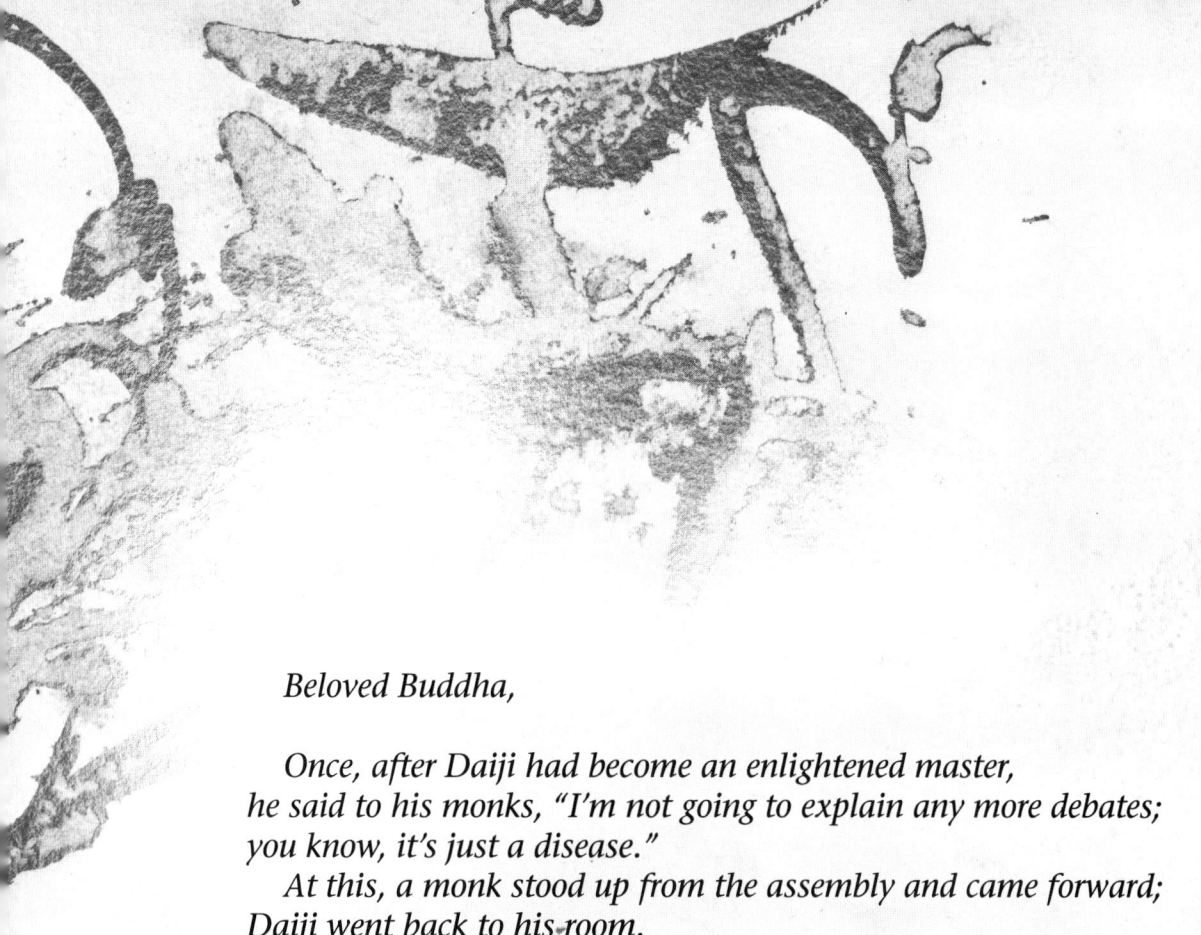

Once, after Daiji had become an enlightened master,
he said to his monks, "I'm not going to explain any more debates;
you know, it's just a disease."
At this, a monk stood up from the assembly and came forward;
Daiji went back to his room.

On another occasion, when Daiji was sweeping the ground,
Jōshū asked him how to manifest prajna.
Daiji repeated, "How can we manifest prajna?"
At this, Jōshū gave a great laugh.
The next day, seeing Jōshū sweeping the ground,
Daiji asked him, "How can we manifest prajna?"
Jōshū put down his broom and laughed aloud,
clapping his hands.
Daiji went back to his room.

NO MIND: THE FLOWERS OF ETERNITY

My Friends and my Fellow Travelers,

I would have loved to use the Urdu words for the same, because they have a depth and a poetry...even the very sound of them rings bells in the heart. The ordinary meaning is the same: my friends, my fellow travelers. But I have a very insistent feeling within me to give you the most pregnant words.

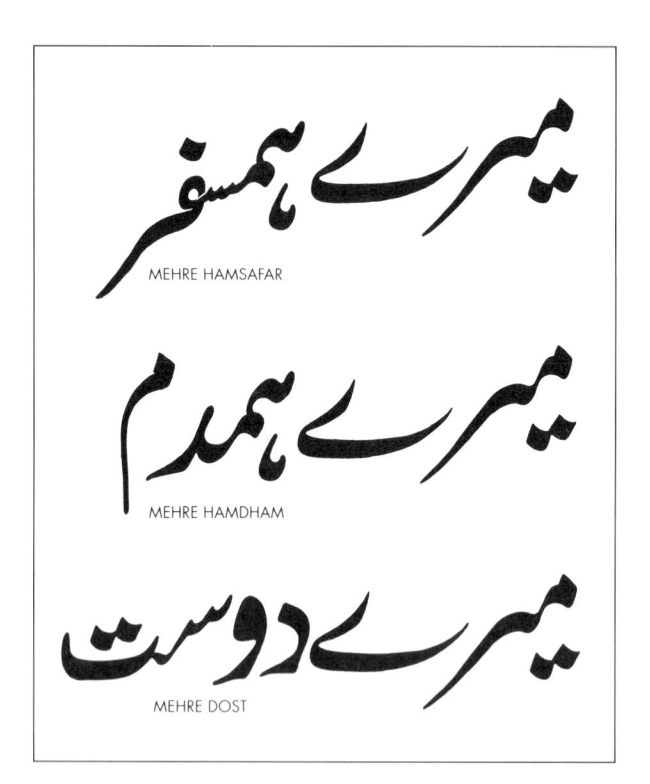

Those words are:

Mehre Hamsafar, Mehre Hamdham, Mehre Dost.

Mehre Hamsafar means "my fellow travelers." *Mehre Hamdham* means "my heart." *Mehre Dost* means "my friend." But such a vast difference....

English has become more and more prose and less and less poetry, for the simple reason that it has been serving scientific and objective technological progress. It has to be definite, it cannot be poetic.

You cannot write mathematics into poetry; neither physics, nor chemistry. Because of this predominant factor of science and technology, English has lost its glamor, its splendor, its music. It has to gain it back, because the objective side of life is not enough. Unless your heart is moved, the words are not very much pregnant with meaning and significance.

These five days have been of immense significance. It can be said that almost never in the history of man has such a phenomenon happened. This has been the deep search of meditators for thousands of years, that once a man becomes enlightened, once a man becomes full of light and knows his own eternity, he disappears into the ultimate, into the cosmos. He cannot come again through the womb of a woman. He has no desires, he has no longings. He no longer has any of the passions which drag human souls again and again to the birth and death cycle.

But once a man has gone beyond all these mind-produced desires, greed, and anger and violence, once one has come to the very center of his being, he is liberated. Liberated from himself, liberated from the body, liberated from the mind. For the first time he understands that the body will be only a prison. Now that his intuition has absolute clarity he can see that the body is nothing but disease and death – maybe a few moments of pleasure, which go on keeping you in the body in the hope that more pleasure... But soon one realizes, if one has intelligence, that those pleasures are very phenomenal, illusory, just made of the same stuff as dreams are made of.

The moment this recognition happens, your life energy simply opens its wings and flies into the open sky of the cosmos, to dissolve into the ultimate.

But Gautam Buddha is an exception.

In the form of a beautiful story, it is said that when Gautam Buddha died he reached the gates of paradise. There was so much ceremony to receive him, but he refused to enter. He insisted, "Until every human being passes through the gates of paradise I cannot come in. It is against my compassion."

At the last moment of his death he has predicted that he will be coming back after twenty-five centuries. Of course, he can come only in one way, and that is to possess somebody's body; the womb is no longer possible for him.

For seven weeks continuously I was witnessing a fire test. Each moment seemed to be the last, and each breath going out was not promising that it would be coming back. In those seven weeks, seven times my heart showed symptoms of failure.

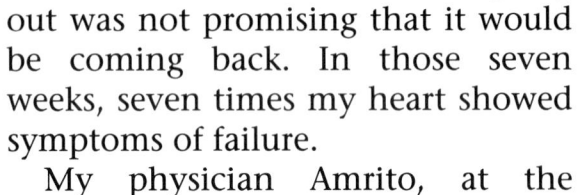

My physician Amrito, at the seventh stroke thought that this was the end. I told him, "The cardiogram can show you how many beats I have missed, but it cannot show you that I am not the heart – I am the witness behind it. And my source of life is not the heart or the body; my source of life is existence itself. I trust in existence, and I trust that this seven weeks' long dark night *will* end."

I would have never told you, but due to Katue Ishida...a woman who has not known me, has just seen my picture and my eyes, and a woman who is a well-known seer and prophetess but rarely speaks. Very rarely people come to her ancient Shinto temple in the forest to ask questions, about their destinies, their future. And most of the time she remains silent; she speaks only when she feels, "Now existence is taking possession of me. I am not speaking, I am only allowing the existence to speak through me."

My Japanese translator, Geeta, has been informing her of everything that has happened in these five tremendously meaningful days. Because of her prophecy that Gautam Buddha has taken possession of my body as a vehicle, I had to admit the truth. But I had also expressed to her that my individuality and Gautam Buddha's individuality are twenty-five centuries apart. He was an individualist – I am a greater individualist. I can be the host, but the guest has to remember that he is not my master.

I have never accepted anybody as my master. It has taken me very long to find out myself, but I am immensely happy that I don't have even to say a 'thank you' to anyone. The search has been absolutely alone, tremendously dangerous.

And there are opinions in which I am bound to differ from Gautam Buddha. Four days he stayed with me, and saw clearly that there is no possibility of any compromise.

Compromise always leads you away from the truth. Truth cannot be a compromise – either you know it or you don't.

Geeta informed Ishida, and she was very much afraid: how will the woman feel? But the woman proved to be of tremendous power. She said, "It does not matter. I love your master and I absolutely agree to whatsoever has happened." And then she suddenly started crying.

Geeta asked her, "Why are you crying?"

She said, "There are no words. For the first time...continuously, for five days, I have been speaking about your master, and I know nothing of him. I have not read his books, I have just seen his eyes, and a door within me has opened and almost like a flood I have been speaking. This is for the first time in my whole life..." She is in a hurry to come.

But the seven weeks' fire, the long night of the soul proved to be a blessing in disguise. It has purified me completely. And these five days of Gautam Buddha as Maitreya Buddha – that was his prophecy, that "My name after twenty-five centuries when I come back again, will be Maitreya the Buddha."

The Friend – Maitreya means "the friend."

It was significant on his part. He was saying, the world of the gurus has ended. The world of the masters and disciples will not be relevant anymore. The master can function only in the capacity of a loving friend. And the disciple has not to be a disciple, has not to surrender to anybody, he has just to listen to the Friend. It is up to him to decide what to do or not. No discipline can be given, no dictation can be given.

In the world of religion this is the beginning of democracy; otherwise, all religions have been dictatorial, fascist, fundamentalist.

I would like you to remember because you have been the witness of all these seven weeks and five days – seven weeks of a constantly deepening darkness, and these five days of the rising sun, of the morning glories, of the birds singing. Again a new beginning, not only in my individuality but also in the individualities of those who have taken the risk to be fellow-travelers with me.

A new dawn, a new man is absolutely needed. Perhaps you are the new man who will destroy all that is rotten and old, that is superstitious and has no roots in intelligence. Perhaps you will be the one to destroy all organized religions, because the moment truth is organized, it dies.

I have heard an ancient story.

A recently arrived devil came running fast to the old devil and told him, "You are sitting here silently, and there on the earth one man has found the truth! It is dangerous for our profession. Something has to be done immediately!"

The old devil started laughing. He said, "Calm down. Cool down, young man! I have made my arrangements already. The scholars, the rabbis, the pundits, the priests – all have reached, and they will organize the truth and that is the most subtle way to kill it. Now they are surrounding the man. They will not allow the man a direct approach to humanity. Humanity has to go through their interpretation, through their commentaries. And that has been, for the whole vast humanity, my way of depriving them of the truth: bring the priest in. The priests are in *my* service!

"All the organized religions, the churches, are in my service. They are China Walls standing between humanity and the ultimate truth."

Just a few months ago the pope has brought into the world a new sin. He has declared that anybody confessing to God directly is committing a great sin; confession has to be through the proper channel, through the priest. You cannot directly start writing letters to God – every letter has to be in care of the priest!

And the letter never goes beyond that. All your prayers, all your confessions never move beyond the priest.

It happened once, a rabbi and a bishop were very friendly. Their friendship was because both loved golf. They had decided to go on Sunday, but the bishop said, "If I am a little bit late, just wait for me in front of the church, because Sunday is a confessional day also, and one never knows how many people are going to confess."

It was getting late and the rabbi started feeling that the line of confessors was so long...he went into the church from the back door, went into the cabin where the bishop listened to the confessions. There was a partition; the confessor was behind the partition. There was only a small window so the priest could hear, and could give him the punishment for his sins.

The rabbi said, "We are getting late. I suggest one thing – I don't know what this confession is, but just do it one or two times and then I will manage. You get ready, and I will finish this line within minutes."

So he watched; one man came and said, "I have committed a rape." The bishop said, "Put ten dollars in the charity box and never do such a thing again. And five 'Hail Marys.'"

The rabbi said, "Don't be worried – you just go and get ready – it is a business matter!"

Another man came and he said, "I have also committed a rape just like the fellow who has gone ahead." But he was not aware that now the bishop was not there.

The rabbi said, "Twenty dollars." The man said, "But I have heard – to the first man you said only ten dollars!"

The rabbi said, "Ten dollars are in advance, so you need

not come to confess and waste time. And ten 'Hail Marys' – now get lost!"

The function of the priest has not been to convert you into the hands of the cosmos. On the contrary, he has been in every way preventing you to open your eyes and see the stars, to open your ears and hear the breeze passing through the pine trees. He has not allowed you to see the beauty of the planet, the beauty of the skies. Neither has he been helpful to take you in your innermost being where is your eternal home. He has been exploiting.

The new man, the new humanity means individual religious people, not organized according to any dogma, doctrine, cult, but simply in tune with existence. And the only way to be in tune with existence is what we have called in the East, meditation, in which no priest is needed. You alone are enough unto yourself.

Maneesha has brought a few beautiful, small Zen anecdotes, dialogues. Just don't get caught into the words, because Zen speaks a totally different language. Alongside the words there is running a constant stream of wordless meanings. Unless you become capable to pass through the word to the wordless you will never be able to understand Zen.

Zen is the purest religion.

It is not an organized church. It respects the individual. It does not have any priests, it does not have any discipline to be forced on you; neither has it any morality that you have to surrender to. It gives you insight and awareness. And through your awareness you have to decide your morality, your responsibility, your discipline, your very lifestyle. It is a

> Every dewdrop
> reaches finally to the ocean,
> and the ocean
> is our ultimate rest.

totally different way of bringing you in tune with the universe.

It teaches you relaxation. It teaches you not to swim against the current – you will never win. Just go with the river, floating, enjoying all that comes on the way: the trees and the stars in the night, and a sunrise and a sunset, and thousands of flowers. And the river...even the smallest river reaches to the ocean. So don't be worried. Big or small, it does not matter. Every dewdrop reaches finally to the ocean, and the ocean is our ultimate rest.

A little biographical note about Daiji, a famous Zen master.

Daiji (780-862) was a famous disciple of Hyakujō. At the age of twenty-nine, he became a monk, and studied both the sutras and the ordinances. He spent some time with Hyakujō, became enlightened, and then made a hermitage on the top of a hill. Later, he went to Mount Daiji, where he expounded Zen, saying, "Six feet of talking is not as good as one foot of doing; one foot of talking is not as good as an inch of doing." He returned to secular life for some time, then shaved his head again, and died as a monk.

He was saying that all this scholarship, all these scriptures, won't help. You will have to *do* something, you will have to dig into your own being. You cannot just like a parrot go on repeating long sutras. They are not going to be your liberation, they are your slavery. Only action with awareness – it does not matter what is the action; the most ordinary action with awareness becomes religious, because it starts having a grace of its own, and a beauty that is transcendental.

To prove this, he himself moved into the ordinary life, into the marketplace, and lived for many years in the marketplace, proving that escaping to the mountains and the monasteries is not the right way. You can go there to learn meditation. Once you have learned it you have to come back to the world to share, to share your enlightenment.

Before dying, he went back to the mountains, shaved his head again, and died as a monk.

A beautiful statement:
"Six feet of talking is not as good as one foot of doing; one foot of talking is not as good as an inch of doing."

The sutra:
Maneesha has asked,

*Beloved Buddha,
Once, after Daiji had become an enlightened master,
he said to his monks, "I'm not going to explain any more debates; you know, it's just a disease."*

All philosophy, all metaphysics, all theology, according to the enlightened ones, is nothing but the disease of the mind, the itching of the mind. If you itch too much, you may bring blood to your own mind, to your own body. It is a disease. Thinking, according to the enlightened masters, is a disease.

It will be good if you try to divide the word disease into its basic roots. It means: dis-ease. All thinking is *dis-ease*. It is a continuous torture inside, a constant rush hour of thoughts running like traffic. And you don't have even a single moment of rest. Even in your nights the thoughts become dreams – more pictorial, more colorful, more enchanting. You become so absorbed....

Perhaps you have never observed: in the day, when you are awake, you may sometimes suspect, "Is it a real world that surrounds me or an illusion, a hallucination, a mirage?" At least the suspicion is possible.

But in the dream you cannot suspect that it is a dream; such is the grip. This state of affairs is not of health, not of wholeness; it is a sickness. It is a dis-ease.

So when Daiji had become an enlightened master, he said to his monks, *"I'm not going to explain any more debates; you know, it's just a disease."*

Get beyond the thoughts and you enter into the world of real health, of real wholeness.

At this, a monk stood up from the assembly and came forward; Daiji went back to his room.

This going of the master to his room simply means, "Go to your rooms and sit in silence." Only in the silences of the heart one has heard the divine, one has felt the divine – never in the thoughts.

On another occasion, when Daiji was sweeping the ground, Jōshū asked him how to manifest prajna.
Daiji repeated, "How can we manifest prajna?" At this, Jōshū gave a great laugh.

Prajna means ultimate wisdom. Naturally Jōshū gave a great laugh – the ultimate cannot be brought to the words, and it cannot be made into explanations. Just asking the question proves your ignorance. And in your ignorance, in your blindness, it is impossible even to indicate to you that the ultimate wisdom is already at the very center of your being, waiting, as a potential to be grown, to be supported, to be nourished. And soon the spring comes and your being starts blossoming into thousands of flowers.

The next day, seeing Jōshū sweeping the ground, Daiji asked him, "How can we manifest prajna *– the ultimate wisdom?"*
Jōshū put down his broom and laughed aloud, clapping his hands.
Daiji went back to his room.

Certainly Daiji has not yet come to the point where he can understand that there are things which cannot be understood, and there are mysteries which remain always mysteries. You can *live* them, you can *sing* them, you can *dance* them, but you cannot explain them.

Who has been able to explain what is beauty? Who has been able to explain what is truth? These mysteries have been experienced by many, by thousands down the ages in all parts of the world – it is nobody's monopoly.

> BLOSSOMS
> ON THE PEAR –
> AND A WOMAN
> IN THE MOONLIGHT
> READS A LETTER THERE.

But still, whenever a man has come to this high peak of consciousness where mysteries are revealed, he immediately understands that there is no way to bring these mysteries down to the ground where explanations are possible, where debates are possible, where philosophical systems can be made.

Those who have known the mysterious, the miraculous, have moved ahead, deeper into the mysteries of existence. The ultimate mystery being the divineness of existence.

Buson wrote:
Blossoms on the pear –
and a woman in the moonlight
reads a letter there.

These small haikus are not ordinary poetry. They simply depict a small scene which has brought some experience of beauty, truth, love, to the heart of the poet.

Blossoms on the pear –
and a woman in the moonlight
reads a letter there...

...And silence abounds.

Maneesha has asked:

Beloved Buddha,
With or without anyone else in residence in You, whatever name we know You by, You are infinitely precious to us. As Katue Ishida said of You, "We must protect this man."
How can we best do that?

Maneesha, if you really want to protect me, the only way is to grow up, to be more mature, to be more integrated, to be more in tune with the dance of the divine.

No ordinary means will be able to nourish me. But if I can see your dance, if I can feel your love, if I can see in your eyes the cool flames of unconditional sharing, you may be able to follow Ishida's indication to save this man.

Now it is time for Sardar Gurudayal Singh.

Mendel Kravitz goes to see Doctor Floss, the dentist.
"Mr. Kravitz," says Floss, "I am sorry to say you need a

complete dental overhaul – side to side and top to bottom. It will cost you five thousand dollars."

"*Sorry? You're* sorry? *I'm* sorry!" cries Mendel. "Five thousand dollars? I cannot afford that!"

"Well," says Floss, "I can recommend another dentist who is sure to be a lot cheaper."

So Mendel goes along to see Doctor Decay who advises him that he did this same job for Solly Saperstein.

"Just call Solly," says Doctor Decay, "and if you are satisfied with what he says, we can arrange something for you."

Mendel phones Solly.

"Ah, yes," says Solly. "My teeth. Well, the dentist did the work some time ago. About two years later I went to stay with my daughter in Hollywood. Yes, she is married to a movie star – lots of money, you can imagine! They were living in a posh hotel in Beverly Hills, with all the comforts. Lots to drink, a room of my own, and I swam in the hotel pool every day. I had it to myself, and I used to swim naked. How about that?"

"That's fine, Solly," says Mendel, "but what about your *teeth?*"

"I am telling you!" replies Solly. "You asked me, and I am telling you!

"One day when I was in the pool, a beautiful young girl dived in. And she had no clothes on. She swam up close to me, I was so embarrassed, I did not know what to do. But she kept smiling, and coming closer and closer. Then she put her hand on me!"

"And *then?*" shouts Mendel.

"Well, then," continues Solly, "for the first time in two years my teeth stopped hurting!"

Big Black Leroy is cleaning the windows on the eighty-third floor of a skyscraper in New York. Suddenly, he loses his balance and falls from the scaffolding, but just manages to catch a window-ledge and hangs there by his finger tips, shouting for help.

"Ah, Lawd!" shouts Leroy, "I'm not ready for them Pearly Gates yet! Save me!"

At that moment, Saint Herbert, the angel, flies out of the sky.

"Hi, Leroy!" says Saint Herbert, hovering beside him. "Have you got faith in the Lord?"

"I sure do!" stammers Leroy.

"Okay" says Herbert, "then I will teach you how to fly. Now, show your faith and take one hand off the window-ledge."

"I can't do that!" stammers Leroy. "No way!"

"Yes, you can," snaps the Saint. "Now, show your faith!"

Turning pale with fear, Leroy closes his eyes and slowly lets go with his left hand.

"That's good, Leroy," says Saint Herbert, patting him on the head, "very good. Now I want you to let go with the other hand."

"Ah, Lawd!" shouts Leroy. "I can't do that!"

"You can do it, Leroy," says Herbert. "Have faith, praise the Lord – and let go!"

Leroy lets go and falls eighty stories to the ground.

"Yup," says Saint Herbert, flying away. "I never did like niggers."

Cardinal Catzass meets his old friend, Buster, from his school days.

"Hello, Buster," says Catzass. "What are you doing these days?"

"I am a logician," replies Buster, shaking hands with the cardinal.

"Really?" replies Catzass. "What on earth is a logician?"

"Well," says Buster, "I am a kind of therapist. I help people by making things clear."

"Really?" says Catzass. "How does it work?"

"Well," replies Buster. "For example – you have a small aquarium in your room, correct?"

"That is amazing!" says Catzass. "Yes I do, how did you know?"

"Never mind," says Buster, "and I deduce that because you have an aquarium, you like fish."

"Amazing!" cries Catzass. "Yes, I do like fish. You are very good."

"Yes, and not only that," continues Buster, "but I deduce that since you like fish, you probably have a fancy for mermaids."

"Amazing!" cries Catzass. "As a matter of fact, I have had lurid fantasies about mermaids all my life."

"And," continues Buster, "because you like mermaids, I deduce that you also like women!"

"My God!" exclaims the cardinal. "I see that you are really an expert. I have a secret lust for women. You are a great therapist!"

Later that afternoon, Cardinal Catzass is in Pope the Polack's private chambers.

"Hey, pope," says Catzass, "I met an old friend of mine today who is a logician."

"Really?" says the Polack. "What is a logician?"

"Well," says the cardinal, "he is a kind of therapist. And he makes things clear."

"Really?" replies the pope. "Like what?"

"I will show you," says Catzass. "For example – you have an aquarium in your room, don't you?"

"No I don't," says the Polack pope.

"Well," deduces Cardinal Catzass, "then you must be a homosexual!"

Nivedano...

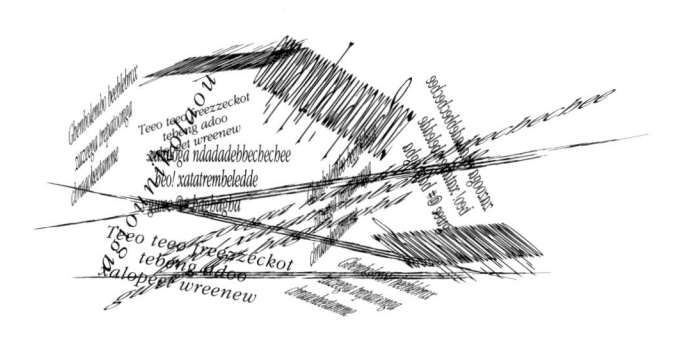

Nivedano...

Be silent. Close your eyes. Feel your body to be completely frozen.

Now is the moment to look inwards with your total consciousness, and with an urgency as if this is going to be your last moment. You have to find your center of being – *at whatsoever cost.*

Deeper and deeper – just like an arrow, go on piercing into the very center of your being. That's where you are a buddha. That's where the doors of all the mysteries of existence open. That's where you come to know for the first time your eternity, your cosmic being.

You are beyond life and beyond death.

What is left? – just a pure witness.

That is the only quality in a buddha – just to be a witness. It is the purest thing in the whole world.

Watch that you are not the body. Watch: you are not the mind.

What remains? – only a witness.

And this witness is your ultimate nature. This witness makes you a buddha.

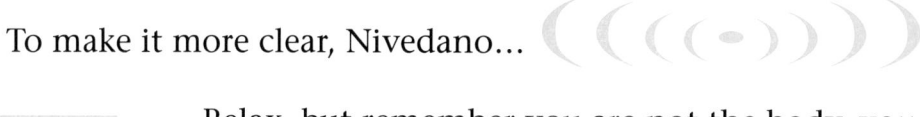

To make it more clear, Nivedano...

Relax, but remember you are not the body, you are not the mind, you are just a pure witness. And slowly slowly a deep joy will arise in you, a blissfulness, an ecstasy, a peace that passeth understanding.

You have come home.

The Buddha Auditorium has become a lake of consciousnesses merging into each other the way rivers merge into the ocean.

The evening was beautiful on its own, but your deepening consciousness, merging into the whole around you, has made it one of the most majestic evenings in the world.

This moment has a splendor, a magic, because you are standing at the very doors
of all the miracles,
of all that is miraculous,
of all that is mysterious.
And all these combined are nothing but different aspects of divineness spread all over existence.
Gather as much silence as you can, as much fragrance as you can. And persuade the buddha to come along with you, so that he is not hiding in the center but comes to your circumference in your activities, in your day-to-day action, in your gestures, in your words, in your silences. When the buddha fills you totally, you have come to blossom. Your potential has become an actuality.

Nivedano...

Come back. But come back not the same person who had gone in.
Come back as a buddha,
with great silence and peace,
with great beauty and grace,
with a heart dancing with joy,
knowing that at the very center of your being
– so close –
is the door to the divine.
A few minutes, just sit remembering and reminding yourself of the golden path that you

have gone on to meet your buddha, and on the same golden path you have come back.

The difference between your circumference and center is lessening every day, inch by inch. The spring is not very far away
when suddenly
your circumference and center
will become one.
That is the moment of enlightenment,
the moment of awakening,
the moment of becoming a buddha.

Okay, Maneesha?
Yes, Buddha.

Truth Has No History
January 2, 1989

Beloved Buddha,

A monk came to see Master Daizui, and said to him, "Mount Gotai and Mount Daizui -- what are they like? How is Mount Daizui?"
Daizui said, "Speak louder – I'm hard of hearing."
The monk repeated the question in a loud voice.
Daizui said: "It is like a thousand mountains, ten thousand mountains!"

On another occasion a monk said, "One of the ancients stood in the snow and cut off his arm. What truth was he seeking?"
Daizui replied, "He didn't cut off his arm."
The monk protested, "He did cut it off! Why do you say that he didn't?"
Daizui observed, "He was enjoying being in the snow."

At another time, a monk bowed to the statue of Manjushri, in the presence of Daizui. The master lifted up his mosquito-flapper and said, "Manjushri and Samantabhadra are both contained in this."
The monk drew a circle, threw it behind him, and then stretched out his arms.
Daizui told the attendant to give the monk a cup of tea.

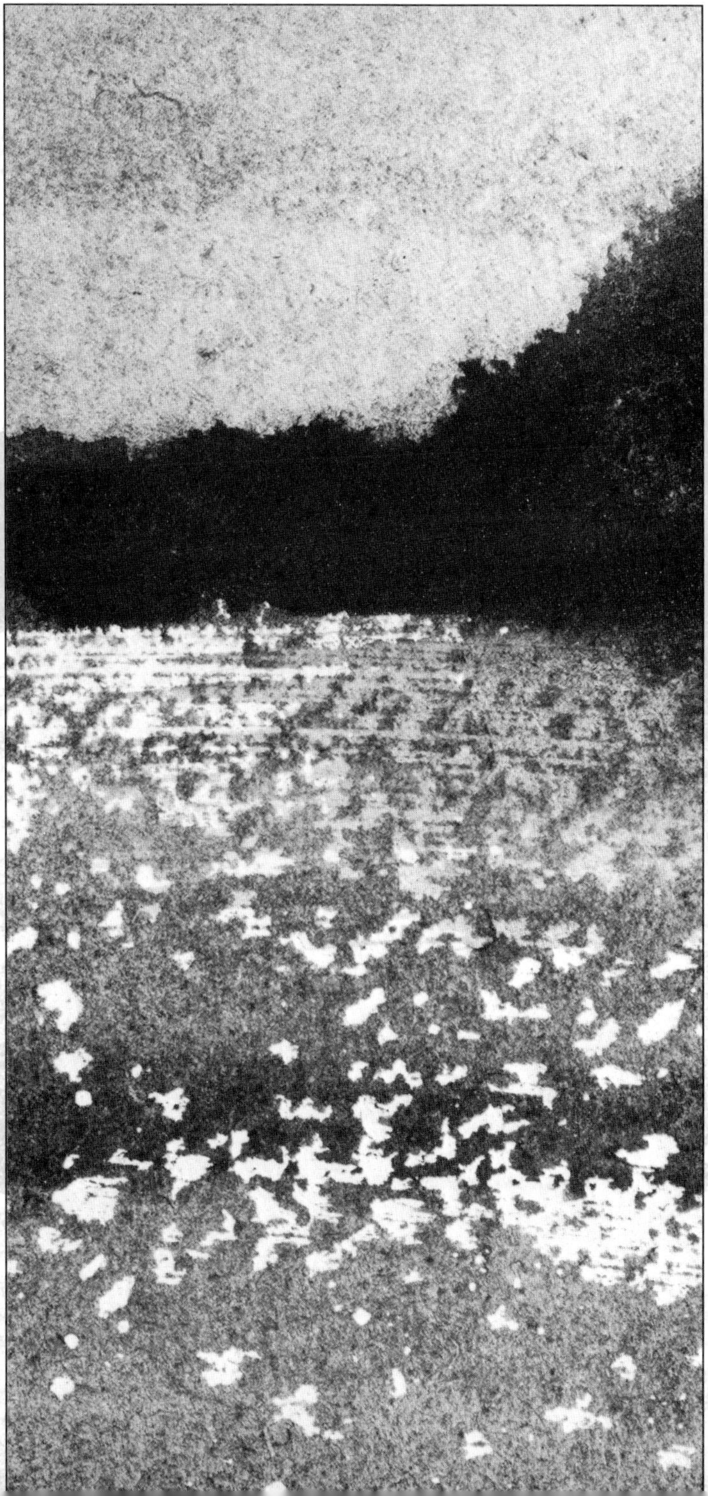

My Friends,

Before I discuss the sutras, a real concern to my heart is more urgent to be discussed.

India's prime minister Rajiv Gandhi has been trying his hardest to create a friendship with China, and it seems they are settling the matter. I don't blame Rajiv Gandhi. Two big countries like India and China cannot remain forever enemies – whoever is weaker, sooner or later is going to give way.

This is the second defeat to India. The first defeat was when China invaded Indian territory in the Himalayas, thousands of miles. India was not strong enough, and particularly it was not ready to fight in the eternal snows of the Himalayas.

Rajiv Gandhi's grandfather – Jawaharlal Nehru, the first prime minister of India – still fought, knowing perfectly well there was no possibility to be victorious. And he was defeated. The Indian armies could not stand the snows of the Himalayas. They had never thought about it; hence they were not prepared.

China conquered Tibet. One of the most significant countries in the world – small and poor, at the highest mountains, it was called "the roof of the world," and it has for centuries been devoting itself only to meditation. A singular country in the whole world – for centuries, continuously, it had only one desire: how to know oneself. It had no armies, it never invaded anyone; it had no desire like that, uncivilized, barbarious. It was primitive, but I will still say Tibet was the most civilized country, the most cultured.

China invaded Tibet – Tibet had no arms, no armies. China crushed the poor Tibetans under machine guns, trampled their monasteries. Dalai Lama, the head of Tibet politically and religiously both, had no other way than to take refuge in the Indian part of Himalayas, in Dharamsala. Since then he has been living there with the thousands of Tibetans who have come with him.

It is a very sad affair to say that nobody in the whole world even protested that an innocent country, which has never invaded and had never shown any desire to invade anybody, should be simply taken over because another country has power. It seems our whole civilization is a pretension; our whole talk about freedom and independence are mere words. Not only that, nobody raised a voice against China. Just now, Rajiv Gandhi has said, "Tibet is China's internal affair."

It seems the law of the jungle still prevails. The bigger fish goes on eating the smaller fish – no protest.

Now Dalai Lama, seeing the situation that India and China are going to become friends, has started to prepare to leave the country – because China's first demand will be that Dalai Lama should be handed over to China; other than that there is no possibility. It has been consistently China's demand that, "Unless you hand over Dalai Lama to Peking there is no possibility of friendship."

And Rajiv Gandhi has forgotten completely those thousands of miles of Indian territory. That too is China's internal affair? Then soon the whole of India will be China's internal affair!

One should not be so weak, either. I would like to say to Dalai Lama: "Don't think of going anywhere; you will not get residence anywhere in the world, because nobody wants to be antagonistic to the biggest country, China." Just two years ago, even America refused just a three-week tourist visa for Dalai

Lama on the grounds that they did not want to annoy China.

I have loved Buddha, and I have loved those who have loved Buddha. I have deep love and respect for Dalai Lama. My suggestion to him is: don't leave this country; just drop the desire to be the sovereign head, the political head of Tibet. In fact, it is not right for a religious man to have such aspirations for being a political head. Just drop that idea. Be an ordinary meditator, a lover of Buddha – then China will not ask for you. You are being asked for because of your continuous desire to be the head of Tibet again. Too much water has gone down the Ganges; it cannot happen, at least in your lifetime.

But my insistence is that fundamentally your desire is wrong. Tibet is gone, out of your hands. You should have renounced it. Your desire for power is a political desire – it is shameful in a man who is thought to be a meditator. Just remain in the Himalayas, and nobody is going to trouble you. The trouble is arising within you because of the desire that you want Tibet to be again under your rule.

Forget all about it. It is ugly, absolutely condemnable, to have such a desire. That was the singular message of Gautam the Buddha: don't have any desire in this world; when the other world, the mysterious world, is ready to open its doors you are asking for some illusory power.

This shows that Dalai Lama himself is not a meditator.

I would like him not to go anywhere. You have a beautiful place in Dharamsala – go inwards. It is time that you prove that there is an inner world far more precious than anything the outer world can give to you. And if you cannot prove this, who do you think is going to prove it?

Once he drops the desire and the claim, and he becomes an ordinary, simple human being, China has no interest in him. He can live in the Himalayas – he is accustomed to living in the Himalayas.

And I say again: nobody is going to behave in a friendly way with you. What can you offer? China offers a tremendous power. You will not get shelter anywhere in the world.

The world is not so civilized as you think. It cares only for those who have power. To be powerful is to be right, and to be powerless...nobody cares about you, whether you are right or wrong.

This has been a tremendous weight on me. In the first place, Tibet is not China's internal affair, and Rajiv Gandhi has forgotten those thousands of miles of Himalayan territory. It is not even mentioned.

And what is to be remembered by Dalai Lama especially: don't get deluded by the so-called talk of democracy, independence, freedom. These things don't exist; the powerful only talk about them. The whole world is still centuries back, living in the same barbarious mind. Only its houses have become better, the roads are better, technology is better, but the man? – it has never been worse than it is now! Because the primitive, barbarian man, howsoever violent, had no missiles, nuclear weapons, atom bombs.

This is the same barbarian man – with modern clothes,

but the mind is as animalistic as you can imagine. And in the hands of these barbarious chimpanzees are nuclear weapons which can destroy this whole earth within ten minutes, with all its living beings. The barbarious man, the chimpanzee, has come to the terminal point where it is going to commit suicide.

I have heard that Ronald Reagan had a great friend, a chimpanzee. He could not find another human being to have a friendship with. The first day of his presidency in America he had gone for a morning walk on the beach with his great friend the chimpanzee.
An old drunkard stumbled around, looking very carefully, and finally he could not resist: he came to these two friends and he said, "President, sir, it does not feel right to have a chimpanzee as your friend."
As Ronald Reagan was going to say something, that old drunkard said, "You shut up! I am talking to Mr. President."

That chimpanzee is hidden in so-called politicians. Wherever there is a desire to dominate there is a chimpanzee hidden within.
I want to repeat again: Dalai Lama has not to go anywhere. It is time to drop the outer desire for domination. Go inwards, you are getting older but you are not growing up. Go inwards to find the kingdom which is not of this world.

Maneesha has brought a few very beautiful anecdotes, sutras, and statements from the history of Zen.

A monk came to see Master Daizui, and said to him, "Mount

Gotai..." it was a great monastery. All these mountains were named after the master who had become enlightened, and because of his enlightenment a thousand seekers had gathered there. Gotai became enlightened and the emperor of China gave the name to the mountain where Gotai had become enlightened – Mount Gotai. And the same happened with Daizui. When he became enlightened the emperor declared, "The mountain should be remembered as a memorial to Daizui and his enlightenment. It will be called Mount Daizui."

> *A monk came to see Master Daizui, and said to him, "Mount Gotai and Mount Daizui – what are they like? How is Mount Daizui?"*
> *Daizui said, "Speak louder – I'm hard of hearing."*
> *The monk repeated the question in a loud voice.*
> *Daizui said: "It is like a thousand mountains, ten thousand mountains!"*

It was a small mountain, but because of thousands of disciples moving on the golden path of becoming enlightened, Daizui said, "It is not only my enlightenment that makes Mount Daizui what it is, but thousands, perhaps ten thousands, are searching the same enlightenment. This mountain is one of the most blessed in the world. So many seekers, so many who are absolutely determined to attain to their potential. A thousand or ten thousand sleeping buddhas are trying to wake up."

This mountain is not a small place. If it can contain ten thousand buddhas, how can it be a small place? It is ten thousand mountains, the whole range that goes for thousands of miles.

The monk could not understand. To understand the statements of Zen masters you have to have some taste of mountains, meditations, masters. You have to have some taste of the spring; otherwise it will look absolutely absurd.

*On another occasion a monk said,
"One of the ancients stood in the snow and cut off his arm.
What truth was he seeking?"*

It is one of the most beautiful incidents in the history of Zen. It happened when Bodhidharma went from India to China, and remained for nine years just facing the wall of a temple. Many came to persuade him, "Why don't you talk to us? We ask questions and you give answers to the wall. It looks very weird."

But Bodhidharma said, "Unless the man comes who has the ears and the heart to understand me, it is better to talk to the wall. At least one is not disappointed." And one day the man came.

He cut off one arm and threw it before Bodhidharma and said, "If you don't turn immediately towards me, I am going to cut my head too."

Bodhidharma quickly turned, and said, "So you have come! I have been waiting for nine years."

Unless a man is ready to stake his very life, the transformation is not possible.

So this monk, asking Daizui, said, "One of the ancients, I have heard, stood in the snow and cut off his arm. What truth was he seeking?"

Daizui replied, "He didn't cut off his arm."

The monk protested, "He did cut it off! Why do you say that he didn't?"

The fact is, he did. But the truth is, he did not.

There was no effort when he cut off his arm; it was as relaxed as if nothing was happening. Hence the truth is, he did not cut it. The fact is, he did cut it. And Zen is concerned with the truth, not with the fact.

Daizui observed, "He was enjoying being in the snow."

He was enjoying perfectly. Even if he had cut his head, he was so relaxed, so trustful. And his search was his absolute determination. For that search,to give your arm or your head does not mean anything. Your arms will sooner or later melt into the earth. Your head, your body will be some day put into the earth.

"So what are you talking about?" Daizui said. "The man did not cut off his arm; he was enjoying it as tremendously as possible." And the turning of Bodhidharma was such a great point in turning his whole being…he became the successor of Bodhidharma.

When Bodhidharma left China to go into the Himalayas and to disappear into the eternal snows… He was getting old, and it was time to search the right place to disappear into the ultimate.

He called his four disciples and asked them, "What is the essence of Buddha's teaching?"

One came forward and said, "To know oneself is the essence of Buddha's teaching."

Bodhidharma said, "You are right, but not enough to be my successor. Just sit down. You have my skin only, you have not gone deeper."

The second man came, and the same question: "What is the essential teaching of the Buddha?" The man said, "Attaining to no-self."

The first had said, "Knowing the self." The second one said, "Attaining to no-self, to nothingness, to utter innocence where the idea of 'I am' does not arise."

Bodhidharma said, "You are better than the first. You have my bones, but you are not yet capable of being my successor."

The third one came before him...the same question. The third one said, "The very essence of Buddha's teaching is silence."

Bodhidharma said, "It is even better than the other two, but not enough to be my successor. If the fundamental and the essential teaching is silence, you should have remained silent rather than using the word 'silence', because the word silence is not silence.

"Your mind is full of thoughts. Beautiful thoughts – thoughts about silence, thoughts about meditation – but all are thoughts. It does not matter whether you are thinking about money or you are thinking about the ultimate truth. Thinking as such is only a disturbance; the object of thinking does not matter at all. You have my very marrow, yet you are not worthy to be my successor."

The fourth man came...the same question. No answer, just tears, and he fell to the feet of Bodhidharma. Bodhidharma declared this man to be his successor.

This was the same man, with one arm. Without saying anything, he has said everything. Those tears were more potent, more expressive than all the words, the whole language, of man. Howsoever philosophically, logically and rationally pronounced, they don't carry the truth, they don't carry love, they don't carry beauty in them.

So it is a truth that the man who cut off his arm was enjoying it immensely. His cutting the arm was very relaxed, in deep trust, in great love. Factually he may have cut off the arm, but in truth he enjoyed the whole experience, the turning of Bodhidharma after nine years to face him.

Bodhidharma had even turned away Emperor Wu of China, calling him an idiot. He had come from the faraway capital to the borders to receive Bodhidharma. And he asked Bodhidharma, "I have done so much religious work, so many fasts. Ten thousand scholars are continuously translating the message of Buddha. I feed millions of Buddhist monks, I support hundreds of monasteries. I have converted the whole land of China to Buddhism. What is my virtue? What am I going to be rewarded by?"

Bodhidharma said, "You idiot! The very desire to be rewarded has destroyed all virtue. You will fall into the seventh hell! And I will not enter into your territory, because you are surrounded by scholars, scriptures, monks, monasteries. I will remain outside and wait for the right man."

It took nine years for him, but his trust... He was growing old, but he waited and waited and waited, and finally the man came.

NO MIND: THE FLOWERS OF ETERNITY

It always comes, you have just to wait – not in a hurry, not asking that he should come right now – just a pure waiting, listening for the footsteps when he comes. He always comes. If there is a right master, thousands of right disciples are bound to come. If there is a pure spring of water, those who are thirsty are bound to come. When the roses bloom, bees come from miles away.

Scientists have been working on the language of the bees, because they have found that bees convey in a certain way a few things. Perhaps they don't have a very long language, alphabetical, but they certainly have some symbols. One bee moves towards the flowers, for miles, and when she has found the flowers she comes back where thousands of bees are waiting and she dances in a certain way. And immediately thousands of bees move in the direction of the flowers. That dance has indicated the direction.

Even bees find flowers, far away. What to say of human consciousness? Those who are alert, those who have a sense of searching some significance in their life, are bound to find where flowers have come to blossom.

So the disciple was, according to Daizui, enjoying. Even by cutting off the arm he was simply offering a present to the master he had found. It was his joy. Hence, as far as truth is concerned it is one thing; fact is another.

Just by the way, I would like to remind you that in the East we have never been writing history. History is an absolutely Western phenomenon. It is with the coming of the British empire that Christian missionaries started writing history about India, but India has never bothered to write history for the simple reason that history will be nothing but facts and facts and facts. And our concern is *truth,* and truth has no history.

Truth is always present; history means the past. Truth is never past. Truth is always here; hence truth cannot have a history. We dropped the whole idea of history.

> *At another time, a monk bowed to the statue of Manjushri, in the presence of Daizui. The master lifted up his mosquito-flapper and said, "Manjushri and Samantabhadra are both contained in this"* – the mosquito-flapper.

Such statements cannot be made anywhere else than in the world of Zen. Manjushri and Samantabhadra are two of the great disciples of Gautam Buddha, who became enlightened while he was alive. Just the story of Manjushri becoming enlightened will suffice you to understand that these people, Manjushri and Samantabhadra, were as valuable as Gautam Buddha himself.

Manjushri used to sit under a tree to meditate, for years. And one day the night was over – suddenly, out of season, the tree blossomed and flowers started falling like rain.

In the East there are such beautiful trees which shower like rain. The one I have loved the most... I don't know which tree Manjushri was sitting under, but most probably this must be the tree – I have loved it from my very childhood. The tree is called *madhukamini*. It blossoms in the rainy season; it blossoms in thousands of flowers all together, and in the night. And by the morning you will find almost a carpet of flowers underneath it, thousands of flowers of such beautiful fragrance. I have not come across another tree like it.

Perhaps Manjushri was sitting under a *madhukamini,* or it

may have been another tree, it does not matter. What matters is, ten thousand disciples of Buddha looked at the tree, looked at Manjushri...could not believe it. It was not the time – what happened to the tree?

Buddha said, "You are seeing only the tree and its flowers. You should look at Manjushri, what has happened to Manjushri. The tree has simply heard it happening to Manjushri. The tree has simply synchronized. If Manjushri can blossom so suddenly, why cannot the tree do the same? Look at Manjushri."

And Manjushri was sitting in silence for seven days continuously, until Buddha himself came to him and told him, "Manjushri, seven days have passed. It is time to get up and tell your fellow travelers what has happened in your being."

Samantabhadra just became enlightened as he looked when Buddha said, "Don't look at the tree, look at Manjushri."

Out of ten thousand disciples only one, Samantabhadra, looked into Manjushri and became enlightened himself. Enlightenment can be a chain effect.

About these two great masters, Daizui says – because one monk was worshipping the statue of Manjushri – "Manjushri and Samantabhadra are both contained in this mosquito-flapper."

Factually it is not so, but in truth, even the mosquitoes which may be caught in the flapper have the same potential as Manjushri and Samantabhadra. That's what Daizui is saying.

Don't think that he is insulting Manjushri or Samantabhadra. He is simply indicating the truth, that "Don't worship the statue. Search for the very source of life. Even a mosquito alive has the essence of being a buddha. It may take millions of years for the poor mosquito to become a human being, but that is not the point to be bothered about."

We have the whole eternity in our hands – beginningless, endless. Somewhere, someplace, one is bound to become a buddha. It is simply a question of your relaxing into yourself.

The monk drew a circle, threw it behind him, and then stretched out his arms. Daizui told the attendant to give the monk a cup of tea.

"A cup of tea" has a totally different meaning when uttered by a master. In Zen, it is again from Bodhidharma. He dwelt on a mountain which was called *T'a,* and he wanted to remain awake twenty-four hours, so he cut his eyebrows and threw them before the temple – it may be fiction, but it is worth mentioning. Rains came and the eyebrows started growing. Those were the first tea leaves.

They are called tea leaves because they first grew on the mountain T'a. And because they are originally the eyebrows of one of the most awakened men, Bodhidharma, tea still keeps you awake. If you don't want to sleep, a cup of tea....

When a Zen master says, "Give this man a cup of tea," he

means a cup of awareness. That is the meaning of tea in the Zen tradition.

A haiku:

*I can't do anything;
my life of contradictions,
blown by the wind.*

I can't do anything...

> I CAN'T DO ANYTHING;
> MY LIFE OF
> CONTRADICTIONS,
> BLOWN BY THE WIND.

In fact anyone who comes to know his innermost silence will agree with the poet who says, "I can't do anything; whatever happens, happens. I am just a watcher at the most."

*...my life of contradictions,
blown by the wind.*

"I can't do anything. Sometimes I am blown to the north, sometimes to the south. It is all contradictory; I am just a witness."

To be just a witness, and not a doer, is the very essence of meditation.

Maneesha has asked a question.

*Beloved Buddha,
During the period of Your being unwell, many of us decided to meditate at the evening video. It seemed time to discover what we had of meditation that was not dependent on Your physical*

presence. So, in a way, while You were passing through Your fire test, we also were being tested. Those few evenings were amazing: a potent silence began to grow – so intoxicating, it was as if You really were with us.

The timing of these two events – was it just a coincidence or did one trigger the other? Was this synchronicity?

Maneesha, you have questioned and you have answered. It was simply synchronicity.

It is time for Sardar Gurudayal Singh.

Down south in Mississippi, Little Black Washington, Little Black Jefferson, and Little Black Lincoln are sitting around comparing their family names.

Little Washington says, "Mah name is *Neon*."

"*Neon?*" ask the other two.

"Yup," replies Little Washington, "because mah Dad invented the *neon* light."

Then Little Lincoln says, "Mah name is *Poly*. Because mah Dad invented *Poly-ester* pants."

Then Little Jefferson shouts, "Mah name is Gonorrhea."

"You not sayin' that your Dad invented *that?*" says Washington.

"No," replies Jefferson, "but he is the southern distributor!"

Charlie Mildew runs into an old friend for the first time in years.

"Morton? Morton Cash, is that you?" asks Charlie. "I hear you have become fabulously rich."

"I can't complain," replies Morton. "I have a townhouse in

the city, a country estate, two Ferrari's, a wife and three kids, several companies, and some good investments."

"Sounds great," says Charlie, "but after all, what can you do that I can't do? We both eat, sleep, and drink – what else is there in life?"

"You call that living?" scoffs Morton. "Me, I get up, have a huge breakfast, then I lie on my verandah. After that I play a round of golf, and come back for a huge lunch. After lunch, I lie on my verandah again. Later, if I feel like it, I get my chauffeur to drive me to a cocktail party. In the evening I have a huge dinner, lie on my verandah again, and then pop out to the theater – then come back and lie on my verandah."

"That's wonderful," marvels Charlie. "And all without working!"

That evening, at home, Charlie tells his wife all about Morton. When he mentions Morton's wife and three kids, Mrs. Mildew interrupts.

"What is his wife's name?" she asks.

"I don't know," replies Charlie. "I think it is 'Verandah'!"

Father Fumble is doing the rounds of his parish in the Oregon countryside, when he decides to drop in on the Fossil family.

Little Freddy Fossil answers the door, and Fumble says, "God bless you, my son. Can I speak to your mother?"

"You can't," replies Freddy. "She has been run over by the tractor."

"Ah! Lord!" gasps Fumble. "Then let me talk to your father!"

"You can't," replies Freddy.

"Really? Why not?" asks Father Fumble.

"Because he has been run over by the tractor," replies Freddy.

"Sweet Jesus!" exclaims the priest. "Then let me see your Uncle Bob!"

"You can't," replies Freddy.

"My God!" cried Fumble. "Don't tell me that he has been run over by the tractor, too?"

"Yup!" replies Freddy.

"Ah! You poor boy," says Father Fumble. "What are you doing here all by yourself?"

"Me?" asks Freddy. "I drive the tractor!"

Nivedano...

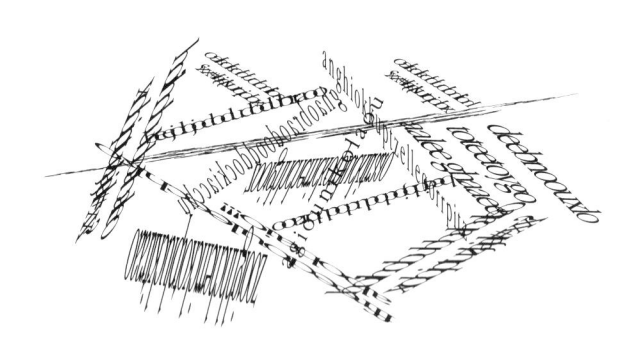

Nivedano...

Be silent. Close your eyes. Feel your body to be completely frozen.

This is the right moment to look inwards with

your totality of consciousness, and with an urgency as if this is the last moment of your life. You are bound to reach to the very center of your being.

As one by one you are reaching to the center of your being, the Buddha Auditorium becomes a gathering of buddhas. At the very center of your being you are a buddha, right now!

Just be a witness, because that is the only quality which remains, ultimately. When the body is gone, the mind is gone, the only thing that remains is witnessing.

Witnessing is your eternal being.

I call this eternal being the buddha.

To make it absolutely clear,

Nivedano...

Relax, but keep on witnessing: the body is not you, the mind is not you. You are only a watcher, a pure watcher. And slowly slowly, all separation between you disappears. This auditorium becomes a lake of consciousness without any ripples. This moment you are the most blessed people on the earth.

The evening was beautiful on its own, but you have added thousands of moons and stars to it. Your splendor is also the splendor of the evening.

This very moment you are entering into the

ultimate, the eternal, the miraculous. The splendor of your being is coming to its spring.

Thousands of flowers will be showering on you. Gather as many as you can, the fragrances, the stars that are falling in your inner sky, and persuade the buddha to come from your hidden center to your circumference, to your ordinary life and activity, to your words and to your silences.

This is the goal: we have to make the center and the circumference to be one.

Only then is your enlightenment.

Nivedano...

Come back slowly, peacefully, showing the majesty of your being and grace, and sit down for a few moments just remembering, recollecting the golden path that you have traveled, the buddha of your innermost world that you have encountered. Something of him will start expressing in your activities.

Remember around the day whenever you can – don't force, just let it come once in a while – and then behave like a buddha, respond like a buddha and you will be surprised how beautiful your actions become, how graceful. Your eyes start shining like mirrors.

Okay, Maneesha?
Yes, Buddha.

TRUTH HAS NO HISTORY

Be Ready to be Chopped
January 3, 1989

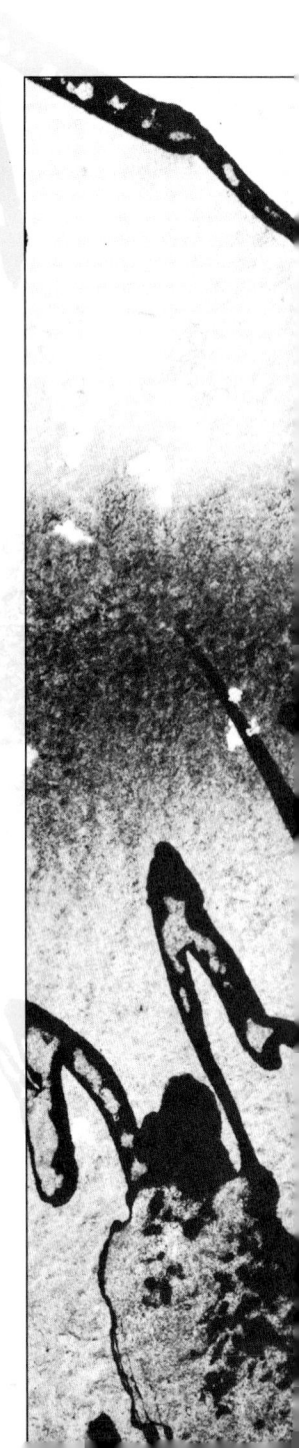

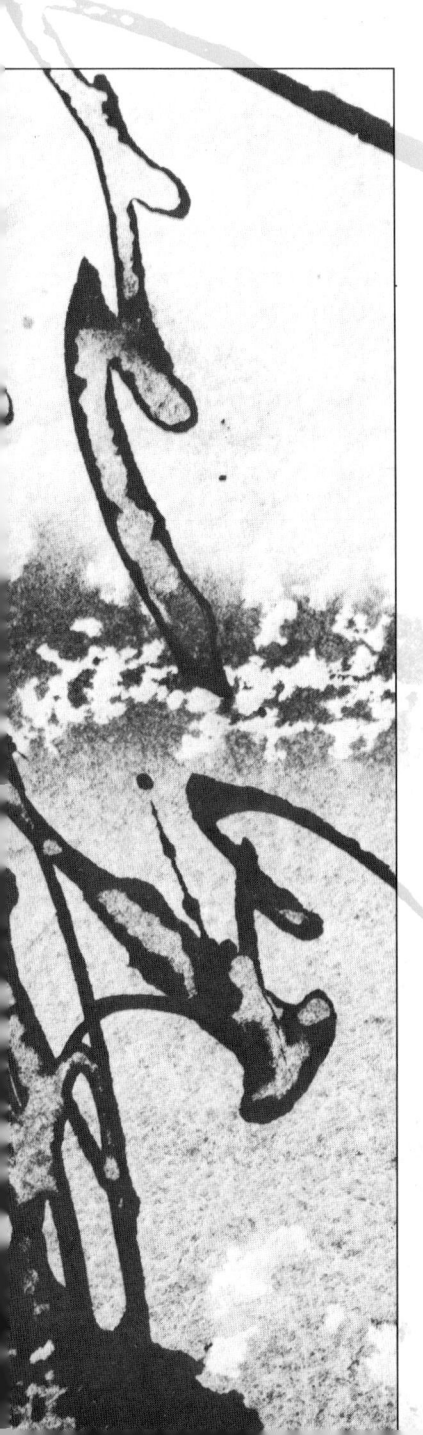

Beloved Buddha,

*Mayoku came to Shōkei carrying his bell staff with him. He circumnavigated Shōkei's seat three times, shook his staff, ringing the bells, stuck the staff in the ground,
and then stood up straight.
Shōkei said, "Good."
Mayoku then went to Nansen.
He walked around Nansen's seat,
shook his staff, ringing the bells, stuck the staff in the ground and stood up straight.
Nansen said, "Wrong."
Mayoku said, "Shōkei said, 'Good'; why do you say, 'Wrong'?"
Nansen said, "Shōkei is 'good,'
but you are wrong.
You are blown about by the wind.
That will lead to destruction."*

My Friends,

I have been waiting to answer a few idiots. I will not mention their names for the simple reason that idiots don't have names – just to be an idiot is enough.

The first idiot was very angry – he is a leader of the sudras who have been converted to Buddhism. He was angry because he thinks that I am a "self-styled buddha."

I call this kind of people idiots because they don't understand a simple thing: Who has styled Gautam Buddha, if he was not self-styled? Who has styled Mahavira, Krishna and Rama? They were all self-styled. Only idiots are born; geniuses have to assert their individuality, they are basically self-styled. There is nothing wrong in it.

But this is the beauty of the idiots: they cannot think. They have never thought, although they have become Buddhists.

In Hinduism there is no such thing as the buddha. In Jainism, the Jaina *tirthankaras* have been primarily called *jinnas,* the conquerors, and secondarily, *buddhas*.

Gautam Buddha tried to be a jinna, because that was prestigious. It was a long heritage, more ancient than Hinduism, because the first tirthankara of the Jainas is mentioned with respect in the ancientmost Hindu scripture, Rigveda. The first tirthankara is called "Adinatha the Jinna."

It was a respectable heritage, and it was a very difficult contest. Eight people were trying to be accepted by the Jainas as their twenty-fourth and last jinna.

Buddha was also one of the contestants. He was being defeated by Mahavira for the simple reason that Mahavira was more masochistic; his whole philosophy was that of self-torture. Buddha could not do that. Being defeated, he immediately grabbed the second word which has been used by

Jainas, which was the 'buddha'. He could not become the Jinna, so he declared himself the Buddha.

Now these idiots of Maharashtra and this small fraction of untouchables converted to Buddhism are condemning me as a "self-styled buddha." First think about your own Gautam Buddha!

The second idiot, also a leader of the converted Buddhists – they are confined only to Maharashtra, a very small minority – has said that if I want to be the Buddha, I will have to renounce all luxuries.

I call these people idiots because they don't know exactly what they are talking about. I will tell you a story about Gautam Buddha; perhaps this will help these idiots to understand.

Buddha renounced in ignorance, not as a buddha. He renounced his palace and kingdom and luxuries, not as a buddha – he was as ignorant as you are. He was in search of light, he was in darkness and doubt. He was as blind as anyone can be. In this blindness, in this darkness, he thought perhaps renouncing the kingdom, renouncing all comforts and luxuries was going to help him find truth.

What relationship is there? If this is the truth, that you have to renounce the kingdom, then how many people have kingdoms? Then the people who don't have kingdoms cannot become buddhas.

And how big was the kingdom? Do you understand? –

there were two thousand kingdoms in India at the time of Buddha. His kingdom was not more than a small *tehsil* – a part of a district.

But when he became enlightened he came back to his palace to see his old father, whom he had betrayed in a way, because he had been hoping that in his old age his son would take over the burden of the kingdom, but instead he escaped. He was coming back after twelve years to ask forgiveness from the old man, and also his wife, and his son who was now grown twelve years...the night he was born was the night Gautam Buddha had escaped from the kingdom.

He had gone to see the face of the child, but the child was clinging to the mother and they were covered with blankets. He was afraid to wake up the wife because she might create some tantrum, and his renunciation of the world might be prevented – or delayed, certainly. So he left from the door without seeing the face of his child.

After twelve years, when he became enlightened, the first thing he did was to go back to his kingdom. The father was very angry, but Buddha stood in absolute silence. When the father had said whatever he wanted to say, when his rage was finished, he looked again at the face of the Buddha – he was absolutely unaffected. When his father had calmed down, Buddha said to him, "You are unnecessarily being angry with me. I am not the same person who left the palace. I am a new being, with eyes to see. I have achieved the ultimate. Just look at my face, my silence; look into my eyes and the depth of my eyes. Don't be angry, I have just come to ask your forgiveness that I had to renounce the kingdom. But I have brought a bigger kingdom of the inner, and I have come to share it with you, and all."

Then he entered into the palace to meet his wife. Of course she was angry...but she also belonged to a big empire. She was the daughter of a far bigger kingdom, and as the daughter of a great warrior she had waited for these twelve years without saying a word. What she said is immensely amazing.

She said to Gautam Buddha, "I am not angry that you renounced the kingdom. I am angry that you did not say anything to me when you left. Do you think I would have prevented you? I am also the daughter of a great warrior...."

Buddha felt very embarrassed; he had never thought about it. Her anger was not that he had renounced the kingdom – that was his business. Her anger was that he did not trust in her, in her love; that he did not trust in her and thought she would have interfered in his renunciation. She was not that type of ordinary woman; she would have rejoiced that he was renouncing the kingdom.

Buddha had to ask forgiveness.

His wife – her name was Yashodhara – said, "For these twelve years I have been carrying only one question to ask to you. And that question is: whatever you have attained – and certainly you have attained something, I can see it in your eyes, on your face, in your grace. My question is: Whatever you have attained, was it not possible to attain it in the palace, in the kingdom? Was renunciation necessary?"

Gautam Buddha said, "At that time I thought so, because for centuries it has been said that unless you renounce the world you cannot find the ultimate truth. But now I can say with absolute certainty, whatever has happened to me *could* have happened in the kingdom, in the palace; there was no need to go anywhere."

This is my answer to the stupid.

I am not an ignorant person. My buddhahood has nothing to do with Gautam the Buddha, and I am not a Buddhist, remember it. Just as Buddha was – call it "self-styled" – I am also an individual in my own right. It has nothing to do with your Gautam Buddha. That's why I have called myself Zorba The Buddha, just to make the distinction clear.

But the idiots can neither think nor can they hear.

The third idiot is a professor belonging to the same converted untouchables. Today he has given a press conference in which he says, "Shree Rajneesh has not been initiated. How can he be a Buddhist?"

Who told him that I am a Buddhist? I am a *buddha,* and it has nothing to do with your Gautam Buddha.

And can I ask the idiot professor – it is very rare – who initiated Gautam Buddha? If he can be without any initiation, why can I not be?

He has also said, "Shree Rajneesh should be an ordinary human being."

That's what a buddha is: an ordinary human being.

But it is strange that in a vast state like Maharashtra only three idiots have spoken. Other idiots must be keeping quiet, knowing that I will chop their heads!

Yes, I am an ordinary human being – but that's exactly what 'the buddha' means. Look into the Buddhist scriptures. To be an ordinary human being is the most extraordinary thing in the world.

But it is not coincidence that all these idiots belong to this small sect of Buddhists. I have known the people who converted these untouchables. These sudras, who have been living in slavery, utter slavery and oppression, for twenty-five centuries, suddenly have become very vocal.

The people who initiated them into Buddhism I have known very well. One was Bhadant Anand Kausalyayan, the other was Bhikkshu Dharma Rakshita. Under the political guidance of Doctor Ambedkar, who was an untouchable, these two Buddhists converted a fraction of sudras. Doctor Ambedkar was from Maharashtra, Bhadant Ananda Kausalyayan lived in Nagpur – which is now part of Maharashtra. But neither was Bhadant Anand Kausalyayan a buddha, nor was Bhikkshu Dharma Rakshita a buddha. Both were *Buddhists*. And to be initiated by Buddhists is nothing spiritual.

Initiation by a buddha may have some meaning, but

initiation by Buddhist scholars can't have any meaning as far as those who know are concerned.

I can see clearly that these people are angry. They are angry against Hindus. But anger is as blind as love. I am not a Hindu, I don't belong to any organization. Now they are enraged against me, not knowing that I have been always favoring the untouchables. I have been a friend to these untouchables, whether they are in the Hindu fold or they have become Buddhists does not matter. Their inferiority complex is tremendous. Perhaps nobody in the whole world carries such inferiority as these people.

It was five thousand years ago that a Hindu scholar, Manu, created the caste system, and for five thousand years Hindus have followed it. Not a single untouchable has the guts to revolt against it.

Just today, the news has come that one untouchable has been selling coconuts before a Hindu temple and suddenly people remembered that he is an untouchable, and he is selling coconuts to people, and people bring those coconuts to the temple. As the word spread, the untouchables were beaten, their shops were burnt....

These people for five thousand years have lived just like animals, cattle. Naturally a deep wound of inferiority has been created in their psyche. Just because they have become converted to Buddhism does not mean that their inferiority complex of five thousand years will be simply erased. It is because of that wound, which is still oozing with pus, that they have spoken against me, a friend.

For a moment I thought all my efforts to support the untouchables, knowing perfectly well that this would bring only condemnation from the Hindus, from the Jainas...when

I saw these people speaking against me, for a moment I thought perhaps Manu was right.

The basis of Manu's whole sociology was that the untouchables are souls coming from past lives who, because of their evil acts are born untouchables. Hence they should not be treated as human beings. Obviously, if you treat people like cattle, they go on collecting as much anger and rage as possible.

Speaking against me – who does not belong to any organized religion, who has declined to be a host to Gautam Buddha's wandering soul...I have to remind them that before making any statements about me they should try to understand my philosophy of Zorba the Buddha. It has nothing to do with your Gautam Buddha. And I am absolutely capable to announce myself as an Awakened One – self-styled!

> *I am absolutely capable to announce myself as an Awakened One – self-styled!*

I am not against luxury, I am not against comforts. I am absolutely in favor of luxury and comforts, because the more a luxurious and comfortable life is available to people, the more meditation is possible, the more relaxation is possible.

But these poor untouchables cannot understand anything except poverty. They are poor and they want others also to be poor.

I hate poverty! I want everyone on this earth to be as rich as possible – in both ways, outside and inside. The Zorba is representative of the outside richness of living, and the Buddha is representative of the inside experience of ultimate splendor.

I am bringing to the world a totally new message; hence there is bound to be misunderstanding. But remember perfectly that anybody who raises his voice against me should support it with evidence and logic – and be ready to be chopped!

Maneesha has brought a few sutras. Before the sutras, a little biographical note:

Mayoku, Shōkei and Nansen were all disciples of Ma Tzu.
Nansen was the eldest and Shōkei a little younger.
Mayoku's date of birth is uncertain, but he is believed to have been the youngest.

The sutra:

Beloved Buddha,
Mayoku came to Shōkei carrying his bell staff with him.
He circumnavigated Shōkei's seat three times,
shook his staff, ringing the bells,
stuck the staff in the ground, and then stood up straight.
Shōkei said, "Good."
Mayoku then went to Nansen.
He walked around Nansen's seat, shook his staff,
ringing the bells, stuck the staff in the ground
and stood up straight.
Nansen said, "Wrong."
Mayoku said, "Shōkei said, 'Good'…"

Shōkei was also a buddha, just as Nansen is. Obviously Mayoku was confused. He said,

"Shōkei said, 'Good'; why do you say, 'Wrong'?"
Nansen said, "Shōkei is 'good,' but you are wrong.
You are blown about by the wind.
That will lead to destruction."

What does Nansen mean? For the same act another master, Shōkei, has said "Good." Nansen, to the same act, says "Wrong."

Repetition is wrong. Whatever he had done to Shōkei was fresh, spontaneous; now repeating it is stale and stinking of death. It is no more the fresh breeze of the morning, no more the fresh opening of a rose.

You will find dry roses in strange places like the Bible. But a dry rose is only a memory, a remembrance, a faraway echo of the real rose who was dancing in the wind, in the rain, in the sun. Whenever anything becomes stale, repetitive, a man of understanding is going to call it wrong. Not only that, if you continue like this you are moving towards destruction, not towards enlightenment, awakening, a rebirth.

Hence, both are right. Shōkei is right – Nansen said, "Shōkei is 'good,' but you are wrong. You have become wrong just because you are repeating the same act, which has become non-spontaneous."

Anything that is non-spontaneous is destructive to the soul. It is not a creative act that enhances your being, that enhances your awareness, that makes your love pure gold. It simply leads you towards the graveyard.

Bashō wrote:

*Winter desolation.
In a world of one color –
the sound of the wind.*

Winter desolation.
In a world of one color – but still something is immensely alive – *the sound of the wind.*

WINTER DESOLATION. IN A WORLD OF ONE COLOR – THE SOUND OF THE WIND.

Even in the fall when the forests become full of dry leaves and trees are standing naked against the sky, everything seems to be just like a graveyard, but still there is something alive. When the wind comes even the dead leaves make such music...even the dead leaves start dancing. Those who can understand, those who can feel, will be utterly astonished at the beauty of the dead leaves. They will also be able to see the beauty of the naked trees without any foliage against the sky. Those naked trees also have a beauty, you just need to have eyes to see. Then everywhere you will find life, love, laughter.

Maneesha has asked the question:

*Beloved Buddha,
What is it to be "grown up?"*

Maneesha, everybody grows old; very few people grow up. Growing old is a horizontal process – just moving in a line. You may reach from the cradle to the grave but you have moved horizontally. You have become old, aged, but your inner being is as deep in darkness as it has always been. Unless you start growing vertically, upwards to the heights of consciousness, you are not growing up.

Our whole education is absolutely unaware of the fact that growing up is a different process than growing old. Even idiots grow old; only buddhas grow up.

The process of growing up is going deeper into your roots. Have you ever considered the fact: the higher the tree the deeper are the roots. A high tree, perhaps two hundred feet, three hundred feet, cannot be supported by small roots; it will fall down. A three-hundred-foot-high tree needs exactly the same balance: three-hundred-foot-deep roots. As is the height, so should be the depth.

If you want to grow up you should think of going deeper into your roots, and growing up will be a by-product of your growing more alert, more silent, more peaceful. The deeper you are at the center of your being, a tremendous transformation takes place. You start growing up to the ultimate heights of consciousness. In those heights you are the buddhas. No initiation is needed – you *know* it.

When you have a migraine, do you need a confirmation from others? Nobody says, "This person is having a self-styled migraine," although the poor person who is suffering from migraine cannot prove it by any argument, cannot

NO MIND: THE FLOWERS OF ETERNITY

prove it with any evidence. But that does not matter. One who is suffering from migraine...even if the whole world says, "Without evidence you cannot suffer from migraine," that is not going to change the situation. The whole world may deny it, but the migraine is there. Only *you* know it.

There are a few things which only *you* know. When one becomes enlightened, there is no need of any witnesses; it is not a question of anybody else confirming it. Your enlightenment is absolutely your experience, you don't need any argument.

Once Ramakrishna was asked, "What is the logical, rational support for your illumination?"

He used the word 'illumination' instead of enlightenment. It is an absolute freedom, one can choose what word he wants to choose.

Ramakrishna said, "I am the argument. If you can understand me, if you can feel me you will know my illumination. It is radiating but your eyes are closed. Now I am not responsible for your eyes. If you want to know me, open your eyes – and not only the outward eyes but the inward too, because my illumination is of the inner."

Maneesha, you are all growing up. And you will know, you will feel every day how you are growing up in your sensitivity, in your awareness, in your love, in your silences of the heart. All these flowers are inner. Even if nobody confirms it, it does not matter. It is nobody's copyright!

Once and for all I want the idiots of this earth to know that I don't need anybody's confirmation. I am a man in my own right, and whatever I know of my inner, except me, nobody has any right even to raise a finger about it! If I say I am Zorba The Buddha, you may accept it or you may not accept it, but you cannot question it.

It is time for Sardar Gurudayal Singh.

The TV announcer appears on the screen.
"Good evening, ladies and gentlemen. We interrupt this program to bring you a news flash from the White House. Nancy Reagan's battle with a stubborn cockroach has landed her husband Ronald in the hospital with severe burns and multiple fractures.

"The details are as follows: Mrs. Reagan stamped on the cockroach, threw it in the toilet and sprayed an entire can of insecticide on it when it refused to die.

"Later, Mr. Reagan, while using the toilet, threw in a lit cigarette, which set fire to the insecticide fumes. The explosion caused serious burns to the sensitive parts of his body. Shortly after that, two staff members who were carrying Mr. Reagan to the ambulance were told how he had been injured. They began laughing hysterically and dropped him down a flight of stairs, which resulted in a broken pelvis and fractured ribs.

"The good news for the evening is that the cockroach walked away unharmed."

Izzy Iceberg, the salesman from "Titanic Insurance," pays a visit to the Kowalski's home. Kowalski is out at the pub, so Izzy is forced to talk to Olga.
"Do you know how much your husband's life insurance policy is worth?" asks Izzy.

But Olga does not understand what he is talking about and just looks at him, blankly.

"Let me put it to you another way," says Izzy, patiently. "Do you know what you would get after your husband dies?"

"Ah! I have often thought about that," says Olga. "Probably I will get a parrot!"

Jesus Christ is walking on his way to Jerusalem one day. Suddenly he sees a man sitting at the side of the road crying.

"What is the problem, my son?" asks Jesus.

"I am blind and I cannot see the beauty of the flowers and the birds in the sky," replies the man.

"No problem," says Jesus, just waving his hand in front of the man's eyes. Suddenly, the man jumps up.

"I can see!" he cries, dancing off down the road.

Two hours later, Jesus comes upon another man sitting beside the road, crying.

"What is the problem, my son?" asks Jesus.

"I am crippled and I cannot walk," replies the man.

"No problem," says Jesus, just waving his hands over the man's legs. Immediately, the man jumps up and runs off into the hills singing.

An hour later, Jesus comes upon another man sitting beside the road, crying and weeping. The man looks perfectly healthy and robust.

"What is the problem, my son?" asks Jesus.

"Ah! Jesus!" says the man, "I am German!"

Jesus sits down and cries too.

Nivedano...

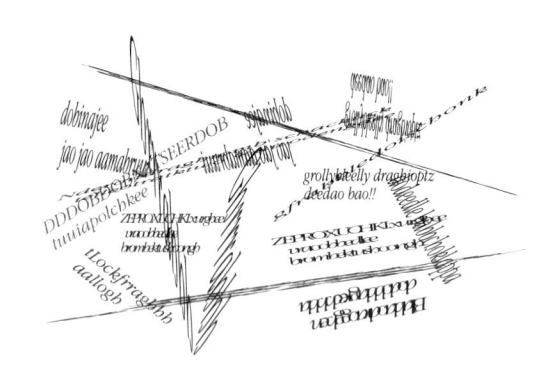

NO MIND: THE FLOWERS OF ETERNITY

Nivedano...

Be silent. Close your eyes, and feel your body to be completely frozen.

This is the right moment to look inwards with your total energy, your total consciousness, and with an urgency as if this is going to be your last moment.

Deeper and deeper.

Go on piercing till you reach to the center of your being. There, you are the buddha.

The only quality that the buddha has is witnessing.

Witness that your body is not you.

Witness that your mind is not you.

Witness that only witnessing is your self nature. This is your buddha. It needs no initiation, it needs only a self-exploration into your own kingdom, the kingdom of your inner being.

Thousands of flowers will start showering on you, and a peace will descend that passeth understanding. A silence will surround you which is almost like a subtle music. A joy will start arising at the very center of your being, like a spring of pure water.

Just witness everything, and remain aloof; don't get identified with anything. You are the unidentified observer of existence.

To make it clear, Nivedano...

Relax, but go on continuing to be a witness. That is the secret word I pass on to you.

The evening was beautiful on its own, but ten thousand buddhas have made it a miracle.

As you relax and just witness, all separation from existence disappears. The Buddha Auditorium becomes a lake of consciousness, awareness, witnessing.

These are the greatest and the highest peaks of human potential. This is what I mean by growing up. Be a buddha, and you are grown up.

Collect as many flowers as you can before Nivedano calls you back. Persuade the buddha, inch by inch. He has been hiding for millions of years at the center of your being. He has to be brought to the circumference also, so that he can become part of your daily, day-to-day activities and affairs.

Nivedano...

Come back. But come back as a new man, a buddha, with the same grace…the beauty, the splendor, the awareness.

Sitting for a few minutes just to recollect, to remember the golden path that you have traveled towards your roots. Remember the joy and the beauty that you have encountered, and remember your original face – I call it the buddha.

Okay, Maneesha?
Yes, Buddha.

When I Call You My Friends, I Mean It
January 4, 1989

Beloved Buddha,

A non-Buddhist scholar, meeting Master Daizui, gave him a bowl. A monk observing this asked Daizui, "What did you use before he presented you with the bowl?"
Daizui said, "I used the one I shall use on my last day on earth."

Once, Daizui was asked, "When all things are annihilated, will That also be annihilated?"
"It will be annihilated," said Daizui.

On another occasion, a monk asked Daizui, "I am told that at the end of the universe a great fire takes place and everything is destroyed. May I ask you whether or not This also shares that fate?"
Daizui replied, "Yes, it does."
The monk went on, "If that is the case, it must be said that This follows others."
Daizui said, "Yes, it does."

The same question was later asked of another master whose name was Shu.
He answered, "No, This does not follow others."
When he was asked "Why not?" the master replied, "Because it identifies itself with the whole universe."

Friends,

The supreme commanding body of Indian Buddhists, Mahabodhi Sabha, has come with a very angry statement in the press against me. I used to think that Mahabodhi Sabha consists of wise people. I was absolutely wrong – it consists of otherwise guys!

The first thing these people should understand: it was not my fault. If you have to be angry, be angry with Gautam Buddha – he knocked on my doors. It is just because I have loved him and respected him that I allowed him to have shelter in my being.

Instead of being joyous, the Mahabodhi Sabha members are angry with me. Perhaps they wanted me to kick Gautam Buddha outright. I did, finally. Now it is a past story.

I have loved Gautam Buddha and I will continue to love him, but these people are better seen from far away. To have them inside you…it was a torture for me, for four days. But just to be polite and nice towards the ancient soul of Gautam Buddha, I waited for the right moment to say goodbye to him. Now there is no need for any Buddhist to be irritated or angry.

And anyway, I have to remind you that it was Gautam Buddha's choice to knock on my doors; I had not asked for it. Your being angry with me is sheer nonsense. It shows that every organized religion becomes a prison even to its own founder – they won't allow him to land again in another body!

Secondly, I had hoped that the people who have been following Buddha would have some compassion, some understanding, some intelligence. It seems they are just as bigoted, prejudiced, as any other organized religion; there is no difference.

It happened with Jesus: the Jews were angry because he was saying that he was the last prophet of the Jews – "for whom you have been waiting for centuries." The high priest of the great temple of the Jews, and the supreme body of the rabbis who decided matters about their religion, decided that this young man Jesus should be crucified. His sin? His crime? – that he was proclaiming himself to be the last prophet.

If you do not agree with him, that is perfectly okay, but there seems to be no reason that he should be crucified.

My case is absolutely different. I am not saying that I am anybody's reincarnation. I hate the very idea! I have my own original face; I don't want to become anybody's carbon copy.

The Mahabodhi Society is saying that I am making statements as if I am the reincarnation of Gautam the Buddha. I have never said a single word about reincarnation. I have simply said that he wanted to use my body – unfortunately I allowed him, but fortunately I was able to persuade him and to say goodbye to him.

Now as far as I am concerned the story is closed. If the Mahabodhi Society wants, it can file a court case against Gautam Buddha! Why did he knock on my doors?

It is not my fault. To be angry at me simply shows your stupidity. If you were really lovers of Gautam Buddha, you would have come here and investigated the case. No one entered these gates to inquire! You could have phoned and inquired, "What is the situation?" But no inquiry has been made at all.

And you are not even up-to-date about the event. That guy you think so much of is no longer here! Next time, if he comes here he will be kicked out, I promise you – to your heart's content!

It is an old, very old story.

The people of Athens could not tolerate the genius of Socrates. In fact, he was the very cream of the Greek mind, but they poisoned him. The little man is always against the giant.

Jesus certainly proved a far bigger prophet than he was claiming to the Jews. After his crucifixion Christianity was born, which is now the biggest religion in the world – almost half of the world is Christian. Certainly, Jesus was not a false prophet. His genuineness is proved by the conversion of half of humanity to Christianity.

But Jews could not tolerate the man – particularly the rabbis, the learned, the scholarly, the people like the Mahabodhi Society of India. They could not tolerate him because if the last prophet is going to be born, he should be born in a high priest's body, or it may take place in some learned scholar, a great rabbi respected by the religion of the Jews. But the last prophet chooses to be a carpenter's son, uneducated, with no claims to scholarship. It was against the arrogance of the scholarly. This simple young man proved to be a great prophet in spite of his crucifixion – perhaps *because* of his crucifixion.

Just today, in a German scholarly magazine, a well-known psychoanalyst has compared me with Jesus. Far away in Germany, that psychoanalyst is more up-to-date about the story that has happened than the Mahabodhi Society. He says, "Just as the Jews could not tolerate Jesus, you will not be tolerated – particularly by the Buddhists." A simple insight....

But I am not claiming to be a reincarnation. I am not claiming anything except that the wandering soul of Gautam Buddha has visited me for four days.

Tathagat, who is the in-charge of this commune – please write underneath "Gautam the Buddha Auditorium," in brackets: "In the memory of his visitation for four days to this commune." Before it and after it, it is none of my concern.

And Maneesha, you should not use only the word 'Buddha'. You should use my full name, "Zorba The Buddha." That way, I am disconnected from every organized religion. I am just myself, and to be myself is not a sin.

I have my own approach to reality. I have said many times that Zorba is half, and Buddha is half. I am a whole human being. I accept the reality of the outer existence, and I love it. And I accept the reality of the inner world. To me, both are one. Neither the inner can exist without the outer – what will be the meaning of the inner without the outer? – nor can the outer exist without the inner; they are two wings of a bird. Only with two wings the bird can fly across the sun in the vast sky of existence.

The sutra:

Beloved Zorba The Buddha,
A non-Buddhist scholar, meeting Master Daizui, gave him a bowl. A monk observing this asked Daizui, "What did you use before he presented you with the bowl?"

> *The little man is always against the giant.*

Daizui said, "I used the one I shall use on my last day on earth."

Daizui's answer is not literally relevant to the question, but Zen has no concern for literal or logical or rational approaches. It takes quantum leaps.

Daizui said, "I used the one I shall use on my last day on earth."

It was a simple thing that has been asked. A non-Buddhist scholar has given him a bowl – Buddhist monks use a bowl for begging. A monk, observing that Daizui has accepted the bowl, asked, *"What did you use before he presented you with the bowl?"*

The reason for his question is that Buddha has given the discipline of non-possession. If you already have a bowl you should not accept another, because it is absolutely useless. Or you should dispose of the first bowl, give it to some other monk who has none – but don't collect things.

That is why the monk asks, "What have you been using up to now?"

Daizui changed the whole dimension of the question. He said, *"I used the one I shall use on my last day on earth."*

He has dropped the idea of the bowl. In fact, he has not been using a bowl. There have been many Buddhist monks who have tried even to improve on Gautam Buddha. They have been using just the hands, like the Jaina monks who don't use a bowl but just their hands. Whatsoever can be contained in two hands cupped together, that is enough for twenty-four hours. Daizui had been following the same discipline, although it is not Buddhist. And he said, *"I used the one I shall use on my last day on earth."*

Once, Daizui was asked, "When all things are annihilated, will That *also be annihilated?"*

By 'That' is meant the inexpressible within you. Nothing can be said except an indication: *That.*
"When all things are annihilated, will That also be annihilated?"
"It will be annihilated," said Daizui.

It is one of Gautam Buddha's most important contributions: the concept of no-self. On this point he rises high above any other religious prophet, tirthankara, shankaracharya. They all stop at the concept of self. Everything will be annihilated, but the self, the *atman* will remain.

In the language that Gautama used, Pali, the self is called *atta,* and no-self is called *anatta.* He preached *anatta;* you will disappear just as dewdrops disappear in the ocean.

Why cling to the idea of self? What will you do with the self when everything is annihilated?

And I agree with him, that at a certain point we were not; then we arose like a wave in the ocean. At some point the wave will be shattered on the rocks on the beach and disappear into the ocean. That seems to be absolutely sensible. You enjoyed your day, you blossomed in the morning with all your glory and splendor, and by the evening it is time to go, it is time to disappear back into the earth, into the cosmos.

No religion has been able to go beyond the self, because to go beyond the self you cannot find many followers. It looks so absurd: all kinds of ascetic disciplines, meditations, yoga, for what? – to be annihilated! Then what is wrong in being just what you are? Why bother, if everything is going to be annihilated? The buddha will be annihilated, and whether you are a buddha or not you will be annihilated too.

According to Indian mythology, which now coincides with the scientific investigations, the whole cosmos, everything, comes out of nothing. Maybe it remains in existence for millions or trillions of years, but a point comes when even the planets, the suns, the moons, even the great stars, get tired and old. It is not only that you die, *everything* that is born, dies. And in the end, this whole existence one day will die completely; there will be nothing except pure space.

That's how it was, some time back: out of nothing, this soap bubble arises, goes on becoming bigger and bigger and bigger. Then at a certain point it bursts forth, and disappears.

Daizui is right when he says, "It will be annihilated."

On another occasion, a monk asked Daizui, "I am told that at the end of the universe a great fire takes place and everything is destroyed. May I ask you whether or not, This *also shares that fate?"*

He has changed his question a little bit, but it makes much difference. First he has asked about *That;* now he is asking about *This*.

Daizui replied, "Yes, it does. 'This' too disappears in the ultimate annihilation."

The monk went on, "If that is the case, it must be said that This *follows others."*
Daizui said, "Yes, it does."

Daizui seems to be very strong, consistent in his observations. He takes his logical conclusion to the very end.

The same question was later asked of another master whose name was Shu.
He answered, "No, This *does not follow others."*
When he was asked "Why not?" the master replied, "Because it identifies itself with the whole universe."

You may think that Shu is giving a different answer. No, he is saying the same thing in positive terms. Because this fellow could not understand Daizui's negative approach, that everything is annihilated... Shu seems to be compassionate and tries the other way round. He says, *"No,* This *does not follow others."*
When he was asked "Why not?" the master replied, "Because it identifies itself with the whole universe."

What is the difference? If the dewdrop disappears, you can call it, in negative terms, the annihilation of the dewdrop. In positive terms you can say the dewdrop has become one with the ocean.
Both are the same answer, but from different angles. Don't think for a single moment that Shu is saying something

different. It is the same, whether the dewdrop disappears or becomes one with the ocean. It is all a matter of what kind of language you love to use.

A haiku:

*Fully rested,
I open my eyes –
Spring.*

FULLY RESTED,
I OPEN MY EYES –
SPRING.

These beautiful haikus say so much without saying anything at all.

Fully rested – utterly relaxed,
I open my eyes – and My God! the spring has come all over.

The spring comes with your relaxation – he is talking about the inner spring. Thousands of flowers suddenly start blossoming. You are filled with fragrances of the beyond.

But be relaxed. And when you are utterly relaxed, in that restfulness become a witness and the spring is always there, ready to surround you from all directions.

Maneesha has asked a question:

*Beloved Zorba The Buddha,
You address us as "My Beloved Friends." Can we really be Your friends or do You call us such out of Your generosity of heart?*

Maneesha, "generosity of heart" will be a humiliation to you, it will be insulting. When I call you my friends, I mean it.

I would have loved to call you something even better, but English does not have something better. Urdu has it: *Mehre Mehbub* – My Love, My Beloved One.

Remember the words – *Mehre Mehbub*.

I say to you, My Friends, My Loves, My Beloved Ones. I mean it. It is not generosity of the heart. Do you understand me? Generosity of the heart will be insulting to you, and I cannot insult you in any way. I love you. *Mehre Mehbub*.

It is time for Sardar Gurudayal Singh.

Mrs. Feigenbaum is having a nap one afternoon when she is awoken by the sounds of loud banging and groaning from downstairs. She creeps fearfully to the staircase and looks over. In the hallway below, she spies her seven-year-old son, Rubin, with a sex manual in his hand. He is standing on the head of six-year-old Ruthie from next door. Both of the kids are naked.

"I don't understand what has gone wrong," says Rubin. "This book says, 'Take off your clothes.' We did that. Then it says, 'The man gets on top of the woman.' I did that" – he's standing on her head! – "'The man gets on top of the woman.' I did that. Where's all the fun in it?"

"I don't know," replies Ruthie, "all I know is, I have got a headache!"

Newton Hooton goes into the "Hog on Ice" restaurant and orders a glass of water. As Walter the waiter puts the glass on the table, Newton picks it up and throws it in his face.

"Ah! I am terribly sorry," says Newton. "I suffer from a rare tropical disease called the 'Heebie Jeebies' and it makes me do all sorts of weird things. Of course I am always *really* embarrassed later."

"Well, that's okay," says Walter, drying his face. "But I think you ought to go and see my psychiatrist friend, Doctor Feelgood."

A few weeks later, Newton Hooton comes back into the "Hog On Ice" and orders a glass of water from Walter. Walter brings the water and places it in front of Newton, and gets the water thrown right back into his face.

"I told you to go and see a shrink!" shouts the waiter.

"I did," replies Newton.

"Well, it didn't do any good, did it?" rages Walter.

"Yes it did," replies Newton, "because now I don't feel at all embarrassed!"

Rabbi Nussbaum and Rabbi Feldman go to the tailor shop owned by Marcus Pinkus and request two black suits. Pinkus hands each rabbi a suit.

"Are you sure these are black and not midnight blue?" asks Rabbi Nussbaum, peering closely at the material.

"Absolutely black, fit for a rabbi!" replies Marcus Pinkus. "Not a trace of blue."

So the two rabbis buy the suits and start to walk up the street.

"You know," says Rabbi Feldman, "I'm a bit worried that these suits from Marcus Pinkus aren't *really* black."

Just then, two nuns approach.

"Quick!" says Nussbaum. "Open the package and compare the suit to the nuns' habit. Nuns always wear pure black, so we'll know for sure!"

Feldman takes out the coat and, as the nuns walk by, he says, "Sister, could you tell me what time it is?"

As she looks at her watch, Feldman quickly places the coat next to her shoulder to make the comparison.

When the nuns reach the convent, the Mother Superior asks if they have anything to report.

"Yes," says one. "We met two men who looked like Jews but who spoke Latin."

"Latin?" asks the Mother Superior. "Since when do Jews speak Latin?"

"Well," says the nun, "I clearly heard one of them exclaim, 'Marcus Pinkus Fucktus!'"

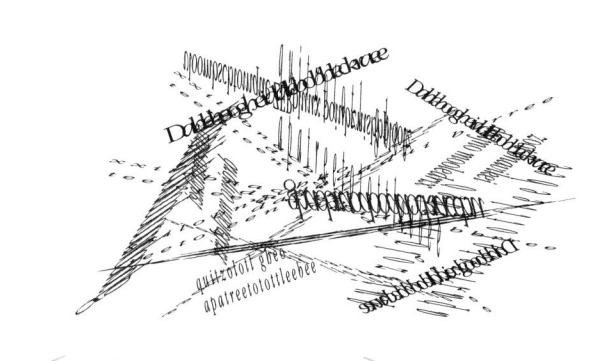

Nivedano...

Nivedano...

Be silent. Close your eyes. Feel your body to be completely frozen.

This is the right moment to look inwards – with your total life force, total consciousness. With an urgency as if this moment is going to be the last moment of your life. With such urgency, it takes just a split second to reach to the center, and at the center you are the buddha.

This beautiful moment...
Ten thousand buddhas utterly silent
and centered in themselves...
Just witnessing that the body is not your being, the mind is not you. Your only quality, your eternal quality is that of a witness. And when I say you are a buddha, I simply mean you are a witness. This witnessing brings the spring into your being.

To make it more clear,

Nivedano...

>Relax.
>Rest.
>Just keep watching, witnessing.
>Slowly slowly, your consciousnesses merge and the Buddha Auditorium becomes a lake without any ripples – of pure awareness, consciousness, witnessing.
>And in the depth of your being arises the spring.
>
>Such a cool, fragrant breeze.
>Flowers and flowers all around –

flowers of eternity,
flowers of love,
flowers of immortality.

Collect as many as you can, and persuade the buddha to come along with you.

The buddha is nobody's monopoly. It is nobody's copyright. It is everybody's innermost being. You don't have to be a Buddhist to be a buddha. To be a buddha transcends *all* concepts of religions; it is everybody's birthright. Persuade it to come along with you, to your daily activities, so everything in your life becomes a meditation, a grace, a beauty, a benediction.

Nivedano...

Come back, remembering you are a buddha. Remembering the grace, the beauty, the silence. Sit for a few moments just to recollect the golden path that you have traveled just now.

And in your day-to-day life remember as much as possible – without creating any tension and anxiety, in a relaxed and restful way – that your every act becomes the act of one who is awakened, of one who has tasted his innermost being.

I want thousands of buddhas around the world, and not a single Buddhist.

I teach you the buddha, but not Buddhism. I hate all 'isms', all religions. My love is for

your eternity, your immortal being.
   I have called that immortal being within you,
"Mehre Mehbub" – My Love, My Friend,
My Beloved One.

   Okay, Maneesha?
   Yes, Zorba The Buddha.

WHEN I CALL YOU MY FRIENDS, I MEAN IT

Beloved Zorba The Buddha,

When Kōkō, a disciple of Jōshū, went to see Master Hōgen, he was asked where he had been recently.
"With Jōshū," he answered.
Hōgen asked, "I have heard about Jōshū and the oak tree; isn't this so?"
Kōkō said, "It is not so!"
Hōgen commented, "But everyone says that when a monk asked about the meaning of Daruma's coming from the West, Jōshū answered, 'The oak tree in the front garden.' How can you say it was not so?"
Kōkō replied, "My master said nothing of the kind! Please do not insult the late master."
Hōgen commented, "Truly you are a lion's cub!"

On another occasion, a man said to Kōkō, "All my life I have killed cows and enjoyed it; is this sin or not?"
"It is not," said Kōkō.
"Why not?" the man asked.
"One killed, one given back," was Kōkō's answer.

Only Creation Shows Your Power
January 5, 1989

My Friends,

One wonders whether we are living in a sane society, or everybody has gone bananas...?

Ronald Reagan has been trying to kill Colonel Kadaffi all these years he has been in power, for no reason at all. Libya is a small, poor country. A few months ago, President Ronald Reagan attacked Libya, and destroyed two houses in which Kadaffi sometimes lives – most of the time he lives in the desert in a tent. But Ronald Reagan killed his daughter and destroyed his houses, for no reason at all.

Just now – this is the last week of his power, but he could not resist the temptation to attack Libya again. He has brought two warships, great carriers; they are standing just close to the shore of Libya, with dozens of fighter planes just waiting for a signal to attack.

Libya simply wanted to see whether they were standing in Libya's territory or in the international ocean. Two jet planes had gone just to look, and they were still inside Libya's territory when the American warplanes immediately bombed the two jet planes of Libya.

The excuse that Ronald Reagan is giving is that Libya is making a factory for biological warfare. He is showing a picture which has been taken from the sky – that means he has already violated Libya's territory; otherwise how could he get that picture?

And the most strange and wonderful and unbelievable thing is, Libya is just making a factory. It has not yet been completed, the building; nobody knows what is its purpose, and nobody asks. *America* decides that it is going to be a factory for biological warfare.

Even if it is going to be a factory for warfare, for biological attacks on other countries, America has the biggest factory like that in the whole world. Ronald Reagan should first destroy the great factory that America has, rather than destroying a poor country's.

You will be surprised to know that President Ronald Reagan and his army chiefs have been denying the fact that they have been using a biological spray on American lands, just to test its potential in case there is a world war based on using destructive biological chemicals. And they have been denying continuously, for years, that it has any bad effect.

But the medical association has come forward to say that it is absolutely wrong: "The president is lying, the army chiefs are lying, because we are the persons who know how many people in these areas have died of cancer – they don't know that they have been killed by their own government!" The rate of cancer in those areas has risen to ten times more than the average. Small children, pregnant women, old men, young men....

And finally – because the medical association has come forward – the president has not answered the medical association; neither have the army chiefs answered. Their silence shows their crime against their own people.

A military war survey from American experts shows that America is the most warlike country in the whole world. In one hundred forty years it has interfered around the world one hundred fifty times, bringing in its military army, attacking poor people, finding any excuse – any excuse is enough. And Ronald Reagan has committed many crimes, for which he is waiting so that the new president can forgive him.

And nobody around the world even objects, even protests. There is absolute silence.

But I have tremendous respect for Libya and its people. I protest, alone, as a world citizen, against Ronald Reagan:

Before you start dropping bombs on others, you should look at yourself.

I have been searching deeply into the American psyche. My understanding is that America and Australia both have been founded by criminals. These criminals were excommunicated from England. They landed, a few of them in Australia and a few of them in America; they became presidents, they became vice-presidents, they killed people without rhyme or reason. Even today in Australia you can hunt human beings.

Something in the very blood of Americans is criminal. And the world has to be aware of these criminals because they have the most power today; it erupts without any cause. Certainly there must be something inside the person when he kills someone without any cause....

Just a few months before, it had become a tremendous problem in San Francisco and L.A. Six persons were shot dead for no reason – just because the traffic was jammed. For miles cars were stopped, nobody knew what was the cause – some accident, some truck has upturned, or what has happened nobody knows. And people started shooting the driver of the car ahead! He was honking as hard as he could, because there were miles of cars ahead – he was absolutely innocent. Seeing this situation, all the car owners immediately started purchasing automatic rifles to carry with them in their cars.

Something deep down in the psyche of the Americans is bloodthirsty. These are the people who have the nuclear weapons, and it needs only to push a button and the whole world will be on fire.

Every action should be taken by the intelligentsia of the world – by the artists, by the poets, by the painters, by the mystics – from all kinds of creative people every protest is needed to save this beautiful planet from bloodthirsty, barbarious people.

America knows only one argument, and that is destruction.

We have to spread the idea that the only real power comes out of creation, not out of destruction. Destruction just shows your madness. Only creation shows your power.

A few more mundane affairs….

The Mahabodhi Society of Buddhists goes on making statements. I have not said a single word against the Mahabodhi Society. Now it is time.

I object to the very name "Mahabodhi." Mahabodhi means "the great enlightenment" – neither in the past nor in the present is a single member of the Mahabodhi Society enlightened. They don't have any right to call their society Mahabodhi; all they can do is to change their name to Maha-*Abodhi* Society of India – *Abodhi* means unenlightened.

Otherwise, they have to show at least a single member, in the past or in the present, who has become enlightened in their Society.

They are just a bunch of rotten scholars, and they have the nerve to threaten me! In fact, I should take them to court; they have to give evidence for why they are calling their society "Mahabodhi."

It is a great word, it has nothing to do with scholarship. I have known many members of the Mahabodhi Society: none of them is even aware what enlightenment is. And they call their society "The Great Enlightenment Society" – how many people have they made enlightened?

People never look at themselves. They don't understand the implications of simple words. Although they are great scholars, they go on reciting the old sutras of Buddha. Most of them are out of date.

I have spoken more on Buddha than anybody in the whole world. I have loved the man; hence I have been choosing only the sutras that can be supported with logic, rationality, and understanding. There are many sutras I have been simply keeping out of my way. If the Mahabodhi Society and the Buddhists of India go on making statements against me, I am going to bring all those sutras that I have kept by the side! I don't care a bit about anybody – Gautam Buddha included.

Just because of my love of the man, because he was not part of any organized religion and he was not inclined to create an organized religion...I have loved his individuality, his grace. But that does not mean that I agree with him one hundred percent. Not more than ten percent is my agreement with his ideas; ninety percent are absolute rubbish. Now these people are provoking me to bring out all that rubbish and condemn it. Unless I do it they will not be silent.

Such is the blindness, utter stupidity.

One *chamar,* a shoemaker, has been converted from the Hindu sudras, the untouchables, and has become a Buddhist. Today he has given a statement, that before becoming a buddha I have to be initiated by him into Buddhism.

That reminds me of a statement by George Bernard Shaw. He has said, "The people who have lived in inferiority for centuries, if you liberate them don't think they will be equal. They will immediately start being superior to you." There is some truth in George Bernard Shaw's statement.

All these Buddhists who are making statements against me have been for five thousand years untouchables. Just a small group in Maharashtra has been converted to Buddhism – not on any religious grounds, but because of a political game of Doctor Ambedkar.

But he was purchased. That shows that a sudra, even if he becomes one of the greatest law authorities, and particularly an authority on constitutionalism, can be purchased very easily. That is one of the indications of an inferior person.

He was purchased by giving him a post to create the Indian Constitution. He dropped and forgot all about Buddhism. And these three hundred thousand people that he has converted have suffered unnecessary injury, because he himself made the constitution not knowing – that is why I say a man of unawareness can do things with all good intentions, but is bound to commit some deep mistake... He made the constitution and he made arrangements for the untouchables: special privileges in schools, in colleges, in universities; a special quota for them because they cannot compete with others. Special quotas in every service of the government. But he forgot completely that it would be applicable only if the sudras remain in the Hindu fold, and he converted these three hundred thousand sudras of Maharashtra to Buddhism. Now they don't have any privileges, no quota, no special scholarships.

Now Doctor Ambedkar has ditched them into a far more inferior, far more difficult life. At least the Hindu untouchables have some privileges, some concessions, some special quotas as a compensation for their oppression for centuries, their suppression and exploitation. But these Buddhists – they have lost that. And the constitution was made by the same man who turned these poor people into Buddhists.

But George Bernard Shaw is right. And these people have remained under slavery, like cattle, just because they have become Buddhists on political grounds.

I repeat it, because Doctor Ambedkar first thought to convert these people, his followers, to Christianity. But a second thought – that in Christianity they will be drowned and he will not be anymore the leader – and he dropped the idea. He had nothing to do with Jesus or Christianity; his whole effort was to remain the leader.

He thought about converting them to Mohammedanism

but it was the same situation. He would not be in a position to be a leader. Then, he found out that there were no Buddhists in India. He could convert these people to Buddhism and remain their leader. Now this was absolutely a political conversion.

But these politically-converted idiots, who don't understand a single word of enlightenment, are making statements against me.

Ishida phoned from Japan to say that I should not take any notice of these people; it is the fate of the giants and the geniuses to be condemned by the little man. She must have been feeling wounded that Buddhists can behave in such a way. She has issued to the Japanese newspapers and magazines a statement, that "It is I who have prophesied. If Indian Buddhists are angry, they should be angry at me." And she has informed that she will be coming here soon to encounter the press, and to encounter the so-called Buddhists. A woman of tremendous courage....

And they go on misinterpreting my statements. I have never said that I am a reincarnation of Gautam Buddha. I am just a reincarnation of myself.

In my past lives I have come across many Gautam Buddhas, but I have never been anybody's disciple. I have searched myself alone, and I declare again that I am just myself, my original face. These Buddhists have no reason to be worried about it. If they want to learn something about enlightenment we will welcome them, but we don't initiate anybody into Buddhism. We *invoke* everybody to be a buddha.

Why Buddhism? Why this long, unnecessary route? When the buddha is already present in you, all that is needed is to call to him loudly, "Come out! You have been hiding inside for too long; it has become habitual. Come out in people's life, in their actions, in their love, in their friendship. Transform them."

This is authentic initiation. It does not come from without; it is a provocation and a challenge to your innermost consciousness.

Maneesha's sutra:

*Beloved Zorba the Buddha,
When Kōkō, a disciple of Jōshū, went to see Master Hōgen, he was asked where he had been recently.
"With Jōshū," he answered.*

Jōshū was one of the most important Zen masters.

*Hōgen asked, "I have heard about Jōshū and the oak tree; isn't this so?"
Kōkō said, "It is not so!"*

In fact, there was an oak tree just before the cottage of Jōshū, and whenever anybody asked, "What is the meaning of Buddhism?" or "What is the meaning of Bodhidharma coming from India to China?" he pointed to the oak tree, meaning, "Why don't you ask this oak tree, 'What is the meaning of your being here? What is the meaning of your spreading the branches and the foliage?'" If nobody asks the oak tree, that simply shows that nature has no meaning; it has only significance.

Remember these two words: *meaning* is logical, mental; it is only a concept. *Significance* is an experience.

What is the meaning of love? If somebody asks you, you will shrug your shoulders. The meaning of love? It is a joy, it is a great experience; it has significance but it has no meaning. A car has a meaning, an air-conditioner has a meaning; things have meanings, but living beings don't have any meaning.

Meaning means some utility. Significance means some beauty, not utility.

It is factually true that Jōshū used to indicate the oak tree in front of his cottage: "This is the meaning of Buddhism." Now let the Mahabodhi Society of India fight a court case against Jōshū! – he is saying the oak tree is the meaning of Buddhism, the meaning of Bodhidharma coming from India to China.

He is right. Existence has no meaning. It has significance, it has fragrances, it has colors, it has beauty, it has splendor. But meaning...?

Meaning is concerned with commodities, and life is not a commodity. Enlightenment is not a commodity that you can purchase in the marketplace.

That which cannot be purchased will not have any meaning; it will have only significance.

But Kōkō denied it on purpose, because people used to

Existence has no meaning. It has significance, it has fragrances, it has colors, it has beauty, it has splendor.

make a laughingstock of Jōshū behind his back – "What kind of master is he? We are asking about the great meaning of Buddha's teaching, and he indicates towards the oak tree. He is nuts!"

To the rational mind it will appear so.

Kōkō was Jōshū's very intimate disciple.

Hōgen is asking, *"I have heard about Jōshū and the oak tree"* – it has become a joke in Zen circles – *"isn't this so?"*

Kōkō said, "It is not so!"

I have told you about the difference between fact and truth. Kōkō is saying, "Factually it may be so, but not in truth. In truth he did not indicate the oak tree, he indicated the life juices in the oak tree which are the same in us."

We are all rooted in the same existence; we are getting our nourishment from the same existence. The oak tree is just a brother, a friend – maybe mute and dumb, but that does not make any difference. Our life sources are coming from the same existence.

> *Kōkō said, "It is not so."*
> *Hōgen commented, "But everyone says that when a monk asked about the meaning of Bodhidharma's coming from the West, Jōshū answered,*
> *'The oak tree in the front garden.'*
> *How can you say it was not so?"*
> *Kōkō replied, "My master said nothing of the kind! Please do not insult the late master."*

He is dead now, and nobody had the guts when he was alive to approach him and argue about the oak tree. Now that he is dead, please don't insult him. You don't understand the meaning of his indicating the oak tree.

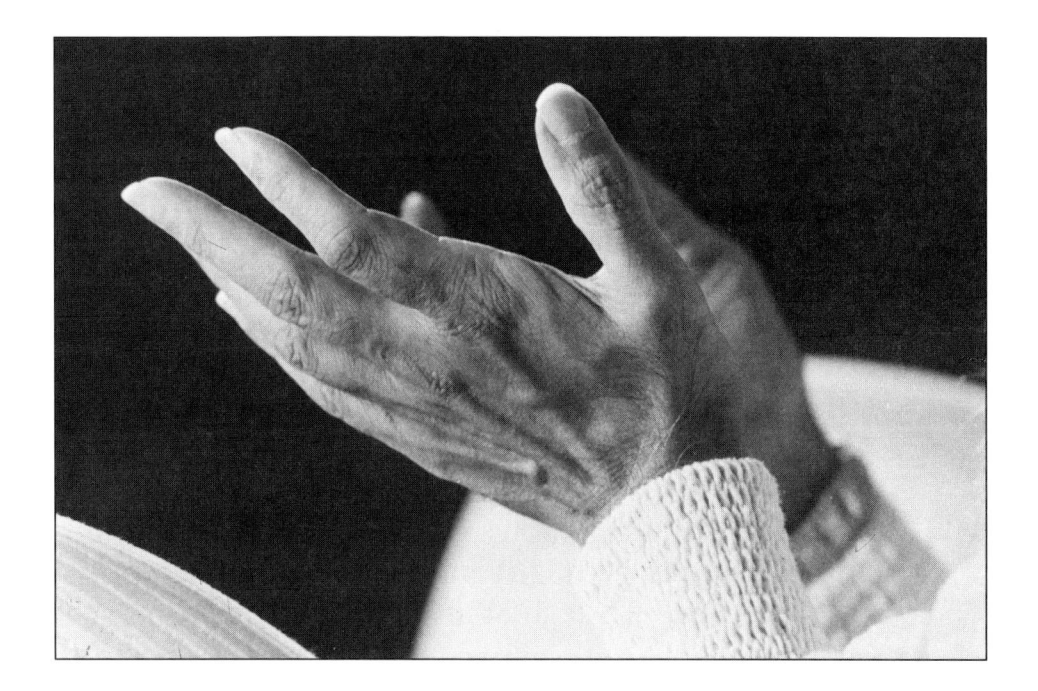

He was not indicating the oak tree, he was simply indicating the hidden sources of life juice rising in the oak tree... *against* gravitation. The oak tree is very strong, very tall, one of the most beautiful trees. Against the force of gravitation, the juices go upwards.

No tree needs a pumping mechanism. *You* cannot bring water from the well without a pump, but the tree is doing exactly that miracle. Every tree is moving juices against gravitation's pull. There are trees three hundred feet tall, and they take up the juices three hundred feet, the waters, their nourishment – to the last leaf, three hundred feet away from the earth. It also gets the same nourishment.

It is a miracle. Jōshū was indicating the miracle, saying that when you also start growing upwards against the gravitation of the earth, when your consciousness starts flying in the sky – when your consciousness becomes an Everest, a high peak of a mountain – you will understand the significance of Bodhidharma's coming to China, or Buddha's meaning.

Hōgen commented, "Truly you are a lion's cub!"

With deep respect – he understood Kōkō's standpoint, that now that Jōshū is dead, nobody should raise the question which was never raised when he was alive.

Hōgen was a famous master, but Kōkō did not care about it. Hōgen respectfully commented, *"Truly you are a lion's cub. You are certainly a great disciple of Jōshū."*

On another occasion, a man said to Kōkō, "All my life I have killed cows and enjoyed it; is this sin or not?"
"It is not," said Kōkō – against the whole tradition of Buddhism.

A master has to respond in the present moment, according to his spontaneity. He does not repeat old scriptures, he does not quote old masters. He has every right to respond spontaneously, and his spontaneous response was very strange, against the whole tradition. He said, "It is not."

According to great masters, there is no sin and there is no virtue. There is only one thing: that is awareness. If you are aware, you can do anything you want and it is not sin. If you are not aware, you may do so-called virtuous acts, but there is no virtue in them. Out of unconsciousness virtue cannot blossom. It blossoms only when you are full of light, full of love, full of consciousness.

Kōkō said, *"It is not."*
"Why not?" – the person was feeling guilty, because the whole tradition says killing cows is a sin.

It was really a part of Hinduism. Buddha was born a Hindu, was conditioned as a Hindu. So even though he became enlightened, some fragments of his old conditioning, of his childhood, remained hanging around him – particularly the idea that to kill a cow is a sin. The man was feeling guilty himself because Buddha has forbidden it, he has propagated nonviolence. And what kind of master is this Kōkō? He says, "It is not."

"Why not?" the man asked.
"One killed, one given back," was Kōkō's answer.

He said, "You cannot really kill anybody; you can only separate the consciousness from the body. So what is the problem? The consciousness, if it still wants to have a body, will enter another womb. You have supported it perhaps, to drop the old body and to get a fresh one. There is no sin in it."

In fact, there is no sin anywhere.

I have to remind you that the original meaning, the root meaning of the word 'sin' is forgetfulness, unconsciousness. It has nothing to do with your actions, it has something to do with your inner remembrance. Who you are, you have forgotten completely.

This is the only sin, to remain unconscious, and the only virtue to become a buddha.

A haiku:

A dragonfly on the rock;
Midday dreams.

> A DRAGONFLY
> ON THE ROCK;
> MIDDAY DREAMS.

I have told you again and again that haikus are not poetries in the ordinary sense; they are poetic, they are more visual than verbal.

Just visualize....

A dragonfly on the rock, having midday dreams....

That is the situation of every unconscious human being. Not only the dragonfly, you are also living in dreams. Until a pillar of consciousness arises in you, you will live in dreams, in nightmares, and your life will be a wastage. It will not come to fulfillment, to contentment, to a deep realization of organic unity with the cosmos.

That is the only splendor to experience.

Nothing is higher than that.

Maneesha has asked a question:

Beloved Zorba The Buddha,
You referred to the Mahabodhi Sabha Buddhists as bigoted and prejudiced. They have also, in essence,

dictated to Gautama and to You how You both should behave. Are bigotry, prejudice and dictatorial attitudes all part of the same syndrome?

Yes, Maneesha.

It is very unfortunate but it has been the whole history of man that the crowd, the mob, the ignorant, has been dictating the behavior *even* of those who have come to be enlightened.

It reminds me of the times of Gautam Buddha. The masses were demanding, "When Mahavira is standing naked under the sun, that is true renunciation. Why are you carrying three pieces of clothing? Just these three pieces of clothing destroy your claim that you are the awakened one."

The masses were asking Gautam Buddha, "Mahavira knows past, future and present. Do you know? If you don't, then you cannot claim to be of the same status as Mahavira."

Nobody ever inquired what Mahavira knows about the future. Perhaps he knows something about the past – he cannot know everything about the past; the past is four million years. Perhaps he knows something about his past lives, that is conceivable; but he cannot know anything about the future.

Do you think Mahavira knew that we would be meeting this evening in Gautama the Buddha Auditorium? Then he must have gone mad! Too much to remember – the whole past, the whole future, the whole present....

Neither Mahavira knew anything about the future nor Buddha knew anything about the future. But to concede... because the problem is, the masses are asking you; otherwise they will not give you the respect.

He conceded, "Yes, when I want to look into the future, I can look. Whenever I want to look at the past, I can. But I cannot say that I know without looking in the past, in the future."

The masses thought, "Obviously he has not attained that great height which Mahavira has attained."

And it is not that they asked only Gautam Buddha; they have been asking everybody, and even your so-called great geniuses have been conceding to their demands, considering the ignorant masses. Otherwise, they lose all respectability.

Perhaps I am the first man in the history of mankind who does not care a bit about respectability. What respectability? – from ignorant people? I don't have to make considerations for anyone. I just depend on my spontaneity and my consciousness. Other than that, I don't care about anybody.

In the commune in America, my friends from all over the world had given me ninety-three Rolls Royces. The whole of America was jealous. Perhaps for the first time they had come across such a man, who owns nothing and yet makes the richest people of the world jealous.

Even Rockefeller was against me, wanted me to be somehow destroyed. Because even the richest could not afford ninety-three Rolls Royces, and I was allowing my friends, if they wanted, to bring Rolls Royces. I had no use for them, I had never gone to look in the garage. Even the Rolls Royce company's president had come to see the garage, because I was a historic customer: never before or after is anybody going to have ninety-three Rolls Royces. And seven more were on the way before they arrested me.

I created so much jealousy. They could not understand, they could not see, they were absolutely blind. They could not see that no man can use even two Rolls Royces together, so there must be something else behind this whole scene.

There was. I was attacking the very egoistic idea of America that they are the richest people in the world – and I proved it. And I still challenge them: if anybody has the guts, just produce ninety-three Rolls Royces.

One bishop was continuously, every Sunday, talking against my Rolls Royces. Such is the blindness! Perhaps he was dreaming only about Rolls Royces; seven days per week he was thinking about it; otherwise how could this become his only sermon? He forgot all about Jesus and the Bible.

And you will be surprised – before I was arrested, there was a rumor for two months continuously that any day I would be arrested. But even the government agencies refused to arrest me, for the simple reason that "You don't have any evidence against that man. If he has ninety-three Rolls Royces, you are free to have more. It is a free country."

The FBI refused; the National Guard refused. The chief of the National Guard simply laughed. He said, "You are just being stupid. Your real reason is jealousy because the commune is living in such beauty and comfort and love and joy. You want to destroy the commune, but I don't see any reason to order his arrest."

They approached the Army – to arrest a single human being who has not even a paper knife. And the chief of the Army said, "You are asking an absolutely nonsense question. Never in the history of man has the Army been ordered to arrest a single human being who has no weapons."

This bishop, seeing that soon I will be arrested because the government and the fundamentalist Christians were determined to destroy the commune, wrote me a letter, saying, "Now that you will be going – it is almost certain – can you give one Rolls Royce to my church in charity?" And this same

NO MIND: THE FLOWERS OF ETERNITY

man, for years, had been condemning them!

I informed him, "I can give you *all* the Rolls Royces. Do you have space in your church?"

He wrote back to say, "No, I don't want ninety-three, because that will destroy *me!* Just one..."

I said, "I am not that miserly. Either ninety-three or none." He became silent.

That shows the psychology of man. What he says may not be what is in his mind; his intention may be totally different. What he acts is not necessarily what he wants to do. The unconscious mind looks all around and follows the crowd.

I love George Gurdjieff – only one man in this whole century – because he said, "Don't consider others." That was his fundamental. Naturally he could not get many followers – not more than twenty lived with him, and perhaps there were two hundred who used to come and go.

Why did he say, "Don't consider others"? Because if you consider others you are considering unconsciousnesses, and if you negotiate with them you are falling down from your own consciousness. Or perhaps you are also an unconscious being, desiring to be respected by the idiots.

I don't consider anybody. It is enough for me to look into myself.

Spontaneity, to me, is the only virtue, awareness the only religion. And only weaklings, cowards, consider others.

Maneesha, it is the same syndrome: bigotry, prejudice, and a dictatorial attitude.

But nobody can dictate anything to me. If this mad society wants to kill me, they can kill me – but they cannot dictate to me.

It is time for Sardar Gurudayal Singh.

When a husband comes home unexpectedly, a French wife says, "Pierre, move over; my husband is home!"
A German wife says, "Fritz, you are two minutes early!"
An English wife says, "Hullo, darling. May I introduce Gilbert?"
A Greek wife says, "Hi, Spyro! The back door is still open!"
An Italian wife says, "Mamma mia, Luigi. If you are going to shoot-a us all, shoot-a yourself first!"
And a Jewish wife says, "Hymie, is that you? Then who is this with me?"

Kowalski decides to take his family on vacation to Miami Beach. He piles everybody into his old Ford and heads on down the Florida highway.
Three days later, he is back.
"What happened?" asks Jablonski, the next door neighbor. "Did you not like Miami Beach?"
"I never got the chance to find out," explains Kowalski. "I was driving down the highway when I came to a big sign that said: *'Miami Beach – Left.'* So I turned around and came back home!"

What is the difference between a misfortune and a disaster?
A great difference. For example: a goat is walking across a bridge, loses its footing and falls into the river. That is a misfortune, not a disaster.
But if an airplane carrying Ronald Reagan and his entire Cabinet crashes, and everybody is killed, that is a disaster – but not a misfortune.

Nivedano...

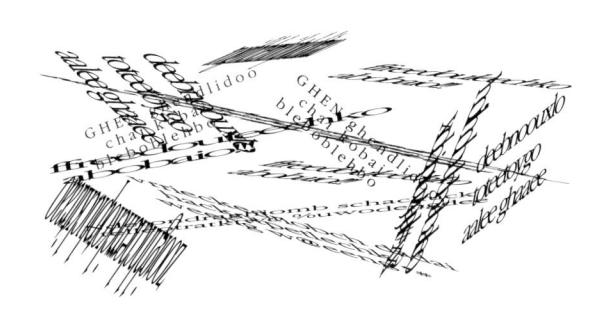

Nivedano...

Be silent. Close your eyes. Feel your body to be completely frozen.

This is the right moment to look inwards with your total consciousness, and with an urgency as if this is going to be your last moment.

The urgency makes the job absolutely easy. Your consciousness rushes like a spear into the center of your being...and there is tremendous silence, a great peace, and an experience of your own buddhahood.

The only quality of the buddha
is just to be a witness.
Watch everything.

Your body is not you, your mind is not you. You are only your witness.

This witness is eternal; it has been always here and will always remain here, whether in some

body or spread all over the universe.
   That's what happens to the enlightened man. When he dies he is not born again; he simply disappears into the vast cosmos, becomes one with it.

To make the witnessing more clear,

Nivedano...

((((-))))

   Relax, but remember only one thing: witnessing. This single word *witnessing* is the master key to all the mysteries and miracles of life.

   The evening was immensely beautiful in itself, but the presence of ten thousand buddhas has made it a splendor, a majesty, a beauty not ordinarily known on this planet. I can see the Buddha Auditorium has turned into a lake of consciousness without any ripples.
   You are the most fortunate ones at this moment on the earth.
   Gather as much silence as you can, as many flowers, that are showering on you – of silence, of love, of joy...
   Gather all the songs that are arising in you, all the dances, and persuade the buddha to come along with you.
   It has been a long time he has been hiding at the center of your being. Bring him to the

circumference of your life. That is the only real test:
> when your actions become graceful,
> when your eyes radiate love, silence, infinity,
> when your silence is a song,
> when you are just sitting, still one can feel
> a dance within you
> of immense beauty and splendor.

Persuade the buddha. It is your own being. Slowly slowly, every day, the difference between the circumference and the center is becoming less and less and less.

The moment the difference disappears you are enlightened.

You don't have any need to be initiated; you don't have any need for any recognition from any authority. You are the authority! You are the buddha!

Just take your life in your own hands.

That is the only dignity of individuality.

Nivedano...

((((•))))

> Come back – not the way you have gone in,
> but as a new man, as a buddha
> with peace, silence and grace,
> with beauty.

Just sit in silence for a few moments to remember, to recollect the golden path you have traveled just now. And remember all that you experience at the center of your being – you have to bring it to the circumference.

You have to remember day and night – without any tension, in a relaxed and playful way – that every act of yours shows compassion and love, that every word of yours shows grace and beauty, that your whole life slowly becomes a song, a poetry…a haiku.

Okay, Maneesha?
Yes, Zorba The Buddha.

Beloved Zorba The Buddha,

*When he first met Sekitō, Hō Koji asked,
"Who is he that is independent of all things?"
Before he could finish his question,
Sekitō covered Koji's mouth with his hand.
At this, Koji underwent an experience
and expressed himself in the following verse:
"Daily, nothing particular,
Only nodding to myself.
Nothing to choose, nothing to discard.
No coming, no going,
No person in purple.
Blue mountains without a speck of dust.
I exercise occult and subtle power,
Carrying water, shouldering firewood."
Later, when he came to visit Ma Tzu, Koji again asked,
"Who is he that is independent of all things?"
Ma Tzu said, "When you have drunk all the water
in the Yangtze River, I will tell you."
At this, Koji underwent another great experience
and composed a second verse:
"The ten directions converging,
Each learning to do nothing,
This is the hall of Buddha's training;
Mind is empty, all is finished."*

Nothing to Choose, Nothing to Discard
January 7, 1989

Friends,

One absolutely innocent man has been hanged yesterday morning. The High Court had no evidence against him – not even circumstantial evidence, not even any technical loophole – but he was sentenced to death because he was the uncle of one of the terrorists who murdered Srimati Indira Gandhi. His only crime was to be the uncle of the man. One simply cannot believe that to be an uncle to a terrorist is enough to hang him.

The Supreme Court has rejected the appeal to reconsider, without giving any evidence or any reasoning why they have rejected the appeal. The president has rejected the mercy appeal without giving any reason why he is rejecting it.

The attorney who was working hard to save this innocent man is my attorney also. I know him intimately; he has been fighting for me in many courts, in many cases. I know his honesty, integrity. His name is Ram Jethmalani. He tried hard in every possible way, saying that there is no evidence; you cannot murder an innocent man. But power is blind, and when blind power becomes revengeful then it is absolutely destructive.

I am not concerned that one man has been hanged. My concern is, as a citizen of this country, that hanging an innocent man is hanging justice itself, is hanging democracy, freedom of individuality, freedom of expression – even freedom to be innocent! And these politicians go on talking about justice and democracy, and under these beautiful names everything corrupt and inhuman goes on, beautifully. Not a single intellectual, or a single freedom lover, nor a single man who would like equal justice for all, has raised any protest.

Ram Jethmalani, as a final effort, approached the World

Court. The World Court said, "Put us in contact with the president." The secretary of the president said, "It is too late" – it was only eight-thirty in the evening – "and we cannot disturb the president at this late hour, and in the morning the man will be hanged." When the man was hanged, Rajiv Gandhi was playing on the grounds as if nothing was happening.

This country has been fighting for freedom – not for *this* freedom. It has been fighting for justice – not for *this* justice, where you don't have any evidence of any kind. You are murdering the constitution of the country, its justice; you are destroying its freedom. And there is no protest.

People are so conditioned to be slaves, that when the whole country should have risen against this criminal act of the Supreme Court and the president of India, there is not even a single sign. It seems the whole country has been castrated.

But I protest with my whole heart!

In the first place, death is not a right way of punishment, even to the person who has murdered somebody. This is the law of the jungle, an eye for an eye. It is not justice. The man has murdered somebody, and you murder the man! Can

> *Power is blind, and when blind power becomes revengeful then it is absolutely destructive.*

blood wash your hands which are full of blood?

And as far as talking is concerned, all the leaders, all the politicians go on talking about beautiful things, giving hope and consolation to the masses, but the fact is that there is *no* law, *no* constitution. If you can murder an innocent man you can do anything – and the country will remain silent.

But I, as an individual, alone, protest this murder of the innocent man.

Secondly, all these past few days I have been exposing Indian intelligence, but nobody seems to come forward and accept the truth. On the contrary, they become angry. Just today I have received from Amaravati a newspaper editorial saying about me, "You are creating your own dictionary" – because I have explained that the word 'bhagwan' is a pornographic word. But the stupid editor does not produce any other meaning of the word from *any* dictionary.

I challenge anybody to produce any other meaning of the word 'bhag'. It means vagina. And you can see in every nook and corner of every city the statue of Shivalinga; it is a phallic statue. It is a man's genitals, based in a feminine vagina, and the whole country goes on worshipping it. Nobody even wonders – what are you worshipping? You are not even ashamed!

Shiva is called by the Hindus not a small god, but *mahadeva* – the great god. And the great god is represented by male genitals. I am not creating any dictionary; I am simply bringing to your notice the authentic meaning of the word, and if you are intelligent, from now onwards nobody should be called Bhagwan – neither Mahavira, nor Buddha, nor Krishna, nor Rama – nobody should be called Bhagwan. It is abusive; it is ugly and obscene.

I had carried that word in front of my name for thirty years just as a challenge, but nobody even came to challenge it. The pundits of this country, the priests of this country, must have understood deep down in their hearts that if they challenged me, I was going to expose the meaning of the word.

Now I have denied even Gautam Buddha, for the simple reason that I don't accept Gautam Buddha as a whole man. He has renounced the world, he has renounced the outer – and a man who is living only with the inner cannot be complete or perfect. Hence, I call myself Zorba The Buddha. But even that is hurting unintelligent people; they don't understand the meaning of Zorba. Even the Sri Lankan ambassador to America has written me a letter, saying that I should not use the word 'Buddha' with 'Zorba'; it is insulting to Buddha.

I wrote him: in the first place you don't have any monopoly over the word 'Buddha'. In the second place, anyone who is awakened has the right to call himself The Buddha, and my effort to bring Zorba and Buddha together is indicative of my whole philosophical approach. I want the world and your inner being to be in tune. The inner and the outer should be balanced.

Zorba the Buddha is my philosophy. But if it hurts, I am helpless.

But I would like my editors not to put it behind my name.

NO MIND: THE FLOWERS OF ETERNITY

I don't want to irritate ignorant, blind, unintelligent people around the world. *You* are my only world; I am living just for you. I renounce the whole world completely.

You should take note of it, Maneesha, that "Shree Rajneesh" is enough to indicate towards me.

As far you are concerned, you can address me as "My Beloved Master."

I have something more important to do than to bother about these idiots. They don't understand even their own scriptures. They are so ugly, they are so pornographic – but they have never read *Shivpuran* or *Vayupuran*. They don't know anything about their own religion, but they get hurt very easily – that shows their conditioned mind. And they have lost all capacity to understand anything new.

I have invited Morarji Desai to the ashram. He has been cheating the owner of the Oceana Building – once I have been in that building with him. He has not been paying, but because he was sometimes chief minister of Bombay, sometimes chief minister of Gujarat, sometimes deputy prime minister of India, and finally he became the prime minister of India, the building owner could not do anything about him. It was at his whim whether to pay the rent or not. Once in a while he would pay.

But now that he is no one, the owner has dragged him to the court, and the court has decided in favor of the building owner. All his followers have simply deserted him. The people who made him chief minister and prime minister – where have they gone? All those *chamchas*... It is a special Indian word; it means all those "spoons" who were sucking his blood – they have all disappeared. Not a single one has invited Moraji Desai to be with him in his house. And he had all the richest people of the country as his friends; they were surrounding him and praising him like anything. Now he has only five hundred and sixty rupees in the bank account, and it is so humiliating that Bombay has collected eleven thousand rupees for him to live – for his whole life.

But I invited him, making it clear that in my campus two conditions have to be fulfilled. You have to stop drinking urine; my people don't like such disgusting habits. And you have to come with a negative AIDS certificate.

One man, M.V. Kamath – one of the oldest journalists, intellectual – immediately reacted, and he gave an interview to a newspaper stating, "I was going to write something good about Bhagwan, but because he has insulted Morarji Desai, now I am not going to write what I was going to write."

Strange...

And yesterday I received his review of my book *Zarathustra* – that's the "something good" he was writing about me. Now, he was in an absolute confusion. He has written such absurd things just to be revengeful, and it has nothing to do with the book *Zarathustra*. If he was angry at me, it was enough that he had shown his anger in the newspapers. But he writes about *Zarathustra* that it is contradictory. He does not give any example – a single example would have been enough – "It is inconsistent," he says, but without any example.

Just because M.V. Kamath says it is inconsistent or self-contradictory it does not become self-contradictory or inconsistent. And he says that there are repetitions in the book. Yes, there are repetitions because it is not a written book. These are lectures, running for months, and one has to understand that a written book is different.

When a person is writing, he can cut; he can remove some passages if there is any tautology, any repetition. He can give the book to a few people to look into to see if they find anything inconsistent. But these are spontaneous talks given to the disciples, and sometimes it is absolutely necessary to repeat a few things again in a different context. They are not repetitions because the context is different.

But just in his own statement, he has made himself a fool – saying, "I was going to write something good," and just because I have invited Morarji Desai, with conditions, he became angry. Because Morarji Desai had made him an international reporter based in Washington. Just to pay him respect, if he was so much offended, he could have invited Morarji Desai to live in his own house!

Now Moraji Desai is hanging... The government had given him a house. First he refused, because it is the opposition who is in power, and he does not belong to this opposition party. To take refuge and support from them he felt was undignified, and he was hoping that he would have so many friends who would come to help him. Nobody has come to help him.

Finally he accepted – this is even more humiliating – the

government's offer to him. Until his death he can occupy a certain bungalow. But that bungalow is already occupied by a woman who used to be the education minister in Chavan's cabinet. Now she is no longer the minister, but she insists she will not vacate the bungalow.

And there are no rules for government bungalows, so she is in a good position. At the most, the government can ask her for the rent, and she is willing to pay the rent. Now there is no way, so the government is searching for another bungalow that somebody can vacate for Morarji Desai. And he is hanging in the air.

Still, because of the courtesy of the owner of Oceana, he has extended, saying to Moraji Desai that "Until you get another bungalow, you can stay a few months."

Now M. V. Kamath was going to write a beautiful press review on *Zarathustra,* but out of anger he writes absolute absurdities.

I was simply amazed that nobody seems to understand the difference between reaction and response. You react with your old conditionings, without ever giving a second thought to any new approach.

Hence, I will be simply my own name. I hope nobody objects to it. Otherwise, I can manage without a name.

I have to live with these blind people and all kinds of idiots, but I am not living for them; they should know. I am living for only *my* people, whose hearts have melted with me.

These few breaths that are left to be here on the earth,
I have to devote to my own people,
with the hope that they will use this opportunity
to become aflame with joy and blissfulness,

to find their roots in eternity, immortality...
to become in their own right
one with the cosmos,
dancing with the stars
and the flowers and the rivers and the oceans.

Maneesha has brought a few beautiful sutras.
First, a small biographical note:
Hō Koji ("Hō" was his family name, "Koji" was a title of respect for a lay student of Zen) first spent time with Sekitō and then went to Ma Tzu. He became enlightened and was one of Ma Tzu's successors.

Beloved Master,
When he first met Sekitō, Hō Koji asked,
"Who is he that is independent of all things?"
Before he could finish his question, Sekitō covered Koji's mouth with his hand. At this, Koji underwent an experience and expressed himself in the following verse....

What must have transpired? Koji was going to ask the question, *"Who is he that is independent of all things?"*

Your innermost being, the witness...but it is not a word, it is an experience.

That's why, before he could finish his question, Sekitō covered Koji's mouth with his hand. "Don't ask such a question which cannot be answered. Don't ask such a question which can only be experienced. Go inwards. Close your mouth, and close your mind. Move into the space of no-mind."

This closing of the mouth was very symbolic, and Koji

went through an experience...and could not believe that such a simple act of a master can manage to ignite a fire within you.

For the first time he saw his own no-mind – the vast space of the inner being.

It is as big as the outer sky; otherwise there will be no balance between the outer and the inner.

He expressed his experience in a verse:

Daily, nothing particular,
Only nodding to myself.
Nothing to choose, nothing to discard.
No coming, no going,
No person in purple.
Blue mountains
Without a speck of dust.
I exercise occult and subtle power,
Carrying water, shouldering firewood.

What he is saying is the experience of every meditator.

Daily, nothing particular...

These words are applicable to you. Nothing in particular, daily, *only nodding to myself.*
When you see your being,
when you see the vast sky,
the freedom, the joy, the blissfulness,
have you ever thought? –

NO MIND

you cannot say anything about it
to anyone.
You cannot say anything about it
even to yourself.
All that you can do is nod your head,
"Yes, this is it."
Nodding, not words.

Only nodding to myself.
Nothing to choose, nothing to discard.

That's what I mean by Zorba the Buddha:
nothing to choose.

Buddha had chosen: he had chosen to escape from the world, he had chosen to leave his wife and child and old father, he had chosen to run away instead of encountering the world and facing the reality. It was a clear-cut choice against the world, against the material, in favor of the spiritual.

A man of totality has nothing to choose. His life is a life of choicelessness. *Nothing to choose, nothing to discard;* they are two sides of the same coin. If you choose something, you will have to discard something.

Nothing to choose, nothing to discard.
No coming, no going, one simply is.
No person in purple.
Blue mountains without a speck of dust.
I exercise occult and subtle power,
Carrying water, shouldering firewood.

"In ordinary life," Koji is saying, "I am exercising what is called 'occult power.' In carrying water, I am being a witness. Shouldering firewood, I am a witness."

NOTHING TO CHOOSE, NOTHING TO DISCARD

And the moment you are a witness you are in meditation. Whatever you are doing or not doing, it is irrelevant.

Later, when he came to visit Ma Tzu, Koji again asked, "Who is he that is independent of all things?"
Ma Tzu said, "When you have drunk all the water in the Yangtze River, I will tell you." At this, Koji underwent another great experience and composed a second verse....

What again transpired?
Ma Tzu said, "I will tell you. First, you have to drink all the water in the Yangtze River – a vast river, it will take eternity for you to drink all the water." Ma Tzu is saying, "Don't ask impossible things."

You are asking the impossible thing which cannot be answered, but only can be experienced. You are asking, *"Who is he that is independent of all things?"* – the witness, the mirrorlike reflecting consciousness. But there is no way to make you understand just by words.

You have to go through the experience of witnessing. That is the only way to dissolve the mystery. Otherwise you can go on collecting answers from masters, from scriptures, from all around the world. But all that you will collect will be simply rubbish.

Anybody else's experience is not going to be your experience. If you drink water, your thirst is quenched, not mine. I will have to drink water to quench my thirst; the experience is absolutely individual.

He recognized the fact that he is asking an impossible question. It is not the master's fault that he is talking of an absurdity:

"When you have drunk all the water in the Yangtze River, I will tell you."

Zen has a way of saying things which nobody else in the world has used. Rather than saying, "You are asking me an impossible question," Ma Tzu says for him first to do something impossible – "Then come and ask me. If you can manage to drink all the water of the Yangtze River, I will manage the experience to be translated into words."

Nothing is possible: neither can you drink all the water of Yangtze...

Immediately, Koji understood and underwent another enlightening experience. He composed another verse:

The ten directions converging,
Each learning to do nothing,
This is the hall of Buddha's training;
Mind is empty, all is finished.

At the very center of your being, ten directions are converging – the whole universe is meeting within you.

Each learning to do nothing,
This is the hall of Buddha's training....

The only thing to be learned is not to do anything, but just *be*. Doing moves you. Doing, in the beginning at least, may take you away from witnessing; you may forget to witness. So in the beginning, just *be* – silent, utterly immobile, as if dead, so that you can experience being in its purity.

Once experienced, you can bring the same quality, the same grace, the same bliss, to your actions in the ordinary life.

Then there is no difference between meditation and life.

NOTHING TO CHOOSE, NOTHING TO DISCARD

Then whatever you are doing is your meditation. If you are not doing anything, *that* is your meditation, because all along, twenty-four hours, you are rooted in your being. You are luminous. Your light, your fire is burning so high that there is no way to forget it. It is radiating all around you. Those who are perceptive, receptive, sensitive, will experience your fire, your life, your song...your dance, even though you are not moving at all.

All that is needed is, mind should be empty. The ultimate experience is the experience of no mind.

Mind is a faculty to work in the world. It has no way to reach to your very center which is far away, back. Mind cannot go backwards, it has no reverse gears; it can only go forward. You can take it to the mountains, to the stars, wherever you want, but you cannot take it to your own being.

If you want to go to your own being, you will have to leave the mind; you will have to go alone. You will have to go in silence, without thought.

And once, just once you know what freedom, what joy, what eternity, what tremendous life bursts forth in you as no-mind is entered, the spring has come to you. Thousands of flowers of eternity blossom. You have come to know the master key which opens all the doors of all the mysteries of existence.

But it has nothing to do with the mind or thinking.

No thought, no mind, no choice – just being silent, rooted in yourself, rejoicing. Thrilled with the experience, overflowing with great benediction to the whole universe – this is the only religion I know of.

All other religions are just frauds.

Hō-ō wrote:

*Sun shower mirrored
in a globe of rain
hangs for one moment,
never seen again.*

Sun shower mirrored in a globe of rain hangs for one moment – he is talking about the rainbow, not mentioning the name. *Sun shower mirrored in a globe of rain hangs for one moment, never seen again.*

Have you ever seen the same rainbow again? Such is our so-called mundane life: just rainbows, the same stuff dreams are made of. There is no need to abandon rainbows – enjoy. But know perfectly well that it is a momentary phenomenon.

I wonder that people like Gautam Buddha, Mahavira and others, have insisted that the quality of the outer world is just like rainbows, dreams, and still they renounce it! Only one thing can be right. Either they understand exactly that the world is just a dream...then there is no point in renouncing it. Do you renounce your dreams every morning? You know they were dreams, it is finished!

But on the one hand they say this whole world is just like dreams, and on the other hand they renounce it and go through all kinds of austerities in renouncing it. Certainly something is wrong. Either they don't understand what they are saying, that the world is just like rainbows... So what? Enjoy the rainbows!

You need not escape from the rainbows. They are beautiful for the moment – why long and desire that they should be permanent? What is wrong in their being momentary?

Just rejoice! When it rains, just dance in the rains.

SUN SHOWER
MIRRORED
IN A GLOBE OF RAIN
HANGS FOR
ONE MOMENT,
NEVER SEEN AGAIN.

When I was a postgraduate student in the university, there was a small street, only for deans of faculties – arts, commerce, science – and renowned professors of different subjects. It was very silent, peaceful, with great trees, ancient trees. It had been a special section built for the British people, so the trees were very ancient, the bungalows beautiful. And the street ended, it did not go anywhere. After a mile of beautiful bungalows and high trees, there was suddenly a stop; you were facing a deep valley. The street was on top of a hill.

Whenever it used to rain, I used to go on that street, because there was no traffic. The last bungalow belonged to the dean of science, a certain Doctor Shrivastava; he was very friendly with me. We used to discuss about the possibility of there being some day a meeting between mysticism and physics – he was a professor of physics, and a world-renowned professor.

But he had never seen...he used to be in the university when I would go singing and dancing in the rain. And I always had to stop at the last bungalow. The last bungalow was his; his wife and his children always waited for me.

NOTHING TO CHOOSE, NOTHING TO DISCARD

Whenever there was rain, they were all standing on the verandah waiting for me. I waved at them and they waved at me...we were not introduced to each other; I did not know that they were the family of Professor Shrivastava. But they thought that I must be mad....

One day Professor Shrivastava said to me, "I want you to meet my family before you leave the university." I said, "I will come along whenever you want." He said, "Why not today?"

So he took me in his car, and he had phoned the family to say, "I am bringing a special guest." The family was waiting for the special guest. When they saw me, they all laughed and ran inside the house!

Professor Shrivastava was very much embarrassed. He said to me, "Forgive me, there seems to be some misunderstanding."

I said, "No, there is some *understanding!*"

He said, "Understanding?" I said, "This is *your* family? We are well-acquainted. They think me mad, I think them mad – we wave at each other..."

He said, "You never told me!"

I said, "I never knew that this was your family."

He took me inside, he called everybody, and he asked, "Why are you laughing?"

They said, "We have been laughing for almost two years! This young man is strange." His wife said, "Whenever it rains, he always comes singing, dancing, alone on the street, and he stops just in front of our bungalow and we wave at each other. We are well-acquainted in a way. We think he is mad, and we know he thinks we are mad, because why should we wait? We wait for hours."

Doctor Shrivastava said, "It is strange. I was thinking to introduce you to my family, but they know you better than me! Why have you never told me?"

I said, "I have been asking many professors to come along with me, it is such a joy, but they say, 'It looks very embarrassing. If some students see, or some professors see, even our jobs can be at risk. You don't have anything to lose, and anyway the whole university thinks that you are a stranger. You can afford it, we cannot.' That's why I did not say anything to you. You are an old fellow, you might not like the idea."

He said, "I like the idea immensely, but I cannot come dancing in the rain – even my family will think, 'My God! That young man has corrupted our father, our husband.'"

I said, "This is my whole business, to corrupt. This was the business of Socrates, to corrupt – this is my business also."

Sun shower mirrored
in a globe of rain
hangs for one moment,
never seen again.

The poet is saying, "Just because it is momentary and you will never come across it again, there is no reason to abandon it. Rejoice in it. The moon, the sun, the rain...they are all so beautiful."

There is no need to renounce anything.

You should be centered in your being; then the whole world is yours. That's why I call my philosophy Zorba the Buddha. Zorba enjoyed everything of the outer world, but he had no idea of the inner. He danced under the rain, he danced on the beach in the full-moon night....

His boss was a thin man, always suffering from headache, stomachache, this or that. And Zorba was a poor servant. One full-moon night, Zorba went to his boss and said, "Boss, only one thing is wrong with you: you think too much. Just come along with me!" And before the boss could have said no, Zorba just pulled him towards the beach.

It was absolutely silent. There was nobody on the beach in the middle of the night, with the full moon showering. And Zorba started playing on his instrument and dancing, and holding the hand of the boss so the boss also had to dance, looking all around to see that nobody is watching.

Finally he got the message. It passed through Zorba's hand. His dance, his joy, his playing on the instrument...something happened to the boss. Zorba left him, and he continued dancing. Zorba went back to the cottage, but the boss continued dancing.

Early in the morning, Zorba came back and said, "Now, come back. Soon people will be awakening."

The boss said, "You have cured me of all my diseases. They were all mind-created. You were right, I think too much. From now onwards I will try not to think. I would also like to see *that* space which opens up when there is no thinking at all."

Zorba was not aware of the inner; he lived in the outer. It is perfectly good, but it is only half.

Buddha lived in the inner; it is perfectly good, but it is only half.

I want to give you the *whole* because to me only the whole is holy; everything else is profane.

Maneesha has asked:

Beloved Master,
You spoke the other night of America – of its being bloodthirsty and destructive. What is the appeal of destruction over creation?

Maneesha, the appeal of destruction over creation is very simple. Destruction needs no intelligence, destruction needs no discipline, destruction needs no education, destruction needs no meditation, no love.

Creation needs intelligence. It needs meditativeness, it needs love – love in its purity. It needs the perceptivity of beauty, it needs the joy of creating something – maybe just a rose bush or a painting, or a small poem, but creation needs your total being to be involved in it. It needs your whole consciousness to be dissolved in it.

Destruction does not require anything of you. Even animals can destroy, even insane people can destroy, even retarded people can destroy. That is the appeal of destruction over creation.

But it is ugly. When you are destroying something, you are also destroying yourself, remember. And when you are creating something – a song, a dance – you are also creating yourself. You are discovering new dimensions of your being.

The more you create, the closer you come to your being, the closer to your potential. Your flights into the open sky...that blissfulness is not available to the destructive person. Only the creative knows the Himalayan peaks of love, of bliss, of splendor...of truth, of beauty, of all that is good, of all that is God.

It is time for Sardar Gurudayal Singh.

It is afternoon at the Washington Zoo.

"Look at that one," says Martha, "the one staring at us through the bars. Doesn't he look intelligent?"

"Yeah," says George. "There is something quite strange about it."

"Yes, he looks like he understands every word we are saying," says Martha.

"Yeah, he walks on his hind legs, too," observes George, "and swings his arms."

"There," says Martha, "he has got a peanut. Let us see what he does with it."

"My God!" says George. "Would you believe it? He knows enough to take the shell off before he eats it – just like we do."

"That other one is a female, isn't it?" asks Martha. "Just listen to her chatter at him. He does not seem to be paying much attention to her, though."

"She must be his mate," says George.

"They look a bit sad, don't they?" asks Martha.

"Yeah, they do," agrees George. "I guess they wish they were in here with us gorillas!"

Paddy and Seamus are in town one day and go for lunch at a smart restaurant. They enjoy a typical Irish seven-course lunch, six beers and a piece of cheese, and receive their bill.

Paddy feels in his pockets for his wallet.

"Ah! B'jesus!" he says, "I have left my money behind. Seamus, can you lend me some?"

Seamus fumbles in his own pockets and then looks up.

"Can you imagine that, Paddy, I've left my money behind too!" he says. "What are we going to do?"

A few minutes later, Paddy and Seamus reach the cashier's table arguing loudly.

"Let me pay for this," says Paddy.

"No!" demands Seamus, "I want to pay!"

They argue for about five minutes in front of the embarrassed cashier, and then Paddy turns to him and says, "Look here – you don't mind who pays for this, do you?"

"No," replies the cashier, "it does not matter who pays for it."

"Well, in that case," says Paddy, waving from the door, "*you* pay for it!"

The Temperature of Marriage:
Wedding Day – one hundred degrees. Feverish.
    Jimmy: "My own sweetie sugarpie."
    Judy: "My own darling honeybunch."

One day later – fifty degrees. Hot.
    Jimmy: "My own precious."
    Judy: "My own love."

Two days later – twenty-five degrees. Warm.
    Jimmy: "Dearest."
    Judy: "Dearie."

Three days later – fifteen degrees. Tepid.
    Jimmy: "Sweetheart."
    Judy: "Dear."

Four days later – five degrees. Cool.
    Jimmy: "Judith."
    Judy: "James."

Five days later – zero degrees. Very cool.
　Jimmy: "Madam!"
　Judy: "Sir!"

Six days later – below freezing. Icy.
　Jimmy: "Bitch!"
　Judy: "Bastard!"

On the seventh day – minus twenty degrees! Very cold.
　Jimmy: *"Get lost!"* – Pow!
　Judy: *"Fuck you!"* – Crash!

Two days after the storm – meltdown.
　Jimmy: "Oh Judy, *Oh! Oh! Oh!*"
　Judy: "Ah Jimmy, *Ah! Ah! Ah!*"

Nivedano...

Nivedano...

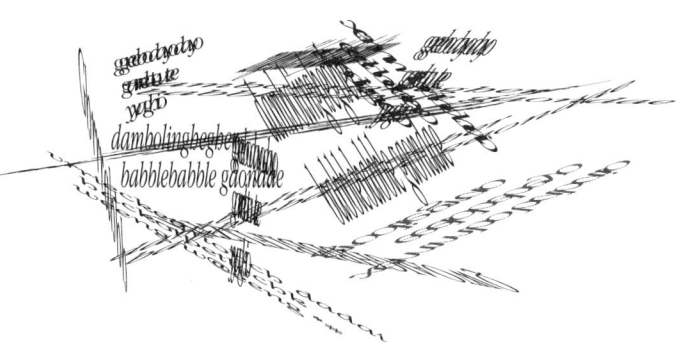

Be silent.
Close your eyes.
Feel your body to be completely frozen.
This is the right moment to look inwards with your total consciousness, and with an urgency as if this is the last moment of your life.
Deeper and deeper...
You are certain to reach to the center of your being – it is not far away.
As you come closer to the center, everything becomes cool, calm, silent.
As you come even closer, everything becomes joyful.
As you reach the center, there is an explosion of light, a tremendous revolution takes place. You have found the eternal in you.
I have been calling this eternal the witness.
From life to life since eternity you have been going on and on, carrying only the witness. Every thing, every life, you have to leave behind; only the witness opens its wings and flies into another life.
Ultimately, when you become enlightened, the same witness flies into the very source of life, disappears, melts down into the universe.
This is *nirvana* – to disappear just like a dewdrop into the ocean.
But for the moment, remember the witness.
You have to live this witness twenty-four hours, without any tension. Whenever you remember, okay; whenever you forget, okay. Slowly slowly,

every moment will become a mirror, reflecting spontaneously the beauty of existence – outer and inner both.

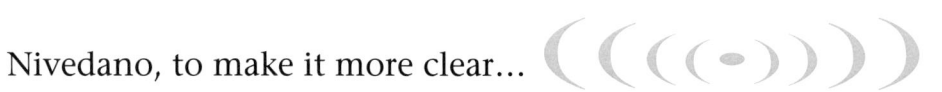

Nivedano, to make it more clear...

((((•))))

Relax.
Rest.
But remember the witness.
You are not the body.
You are not the mind.
You are just the witness, and suddenly flowers start raining on you. A great ecstasy takes over; as you relax, all separation disappears.
Gautama the Buddha Auditorium has become this moment
just a lake of consciousness
without any ripples,
reflecting the faraway stars.
You are the most fortunate human beings at this moment upon the whole planet earth, because you are at your center. This is the most precious, the greatest glory and splendor one can find in life, in existence.
Collect as much joy, bliss, ecstasy...
And persuade the center, the witness, to come along with you.
The witness has to become your very life.
That very moment you will be awakened, you will be the buddha.

Nivedano...

Come back, but peacefully, silently, gracefully.
Sit down for a few moments, remembering the golden path you have traveled, and reminding yourself that the experience of witnessing at the center of your being has to become your very life.
Drawing water from the well,
chopping wood – whatever you are doing,
you have to remember
that you are only a witness.
Nothing has to be renounced,
nothing has to be chosen.
Choicelessly, relaxed,
live both sides of your being:
the outer and the inner.
Be Zorba the Buddha!

Okay, Maneesha?
Yes, Beloved Master.

You Need Two Wings
January 10, 1989

Over the years, the Master has managed to expose the falsities and blind spots of virtually all organized religions in the world. These past few days, it has been the Buddhists' turn to have a look around in the light.

It seems that at least for some, it was too bright for their eyes.

What follows is an excerpt from the Master's discourse of January 10, when He responded to the actions taken by one of the Buddhist organizations in India.

Further developments and details can be found in the book,
Zen: The Mystery and the Poetry of the Beyond.
—*Ed.*

The Dalit Elevation Republic Party of India is an organization of the neo-Buddhists – it has sent a resolution to the government of India that action should be taken against me because I have been comparing myself with Buddha.

In the first place, I have never compared myself with Gautam Buddha. I have always said definitively that he is life-negative, and I am absolutely life-affirmative. There is no possibility of any comparison.

He is a bullock cart, and you want it to be compared with my Rolls Royce? Of course, the basic principle of a bullock cart is the same – the four wheels – but still you cannot compare it with a Rolls Royce.

This organization has told the government that their religious feelings are very much hurt.

In the first place, if you understand religion...it is in the transcendence of thoughts and feelings. There are no religious feelings at all! Only idiots have religious feelings.

I have loved Buddha, just as I would have loved the inventor of a bullock cart; it was a great revolution. Buddha is the beginning of a great revolution, but only the beginning, not the end. Looking backwards, I can see he managed a little bit to go against the tradition, but not wholeheartedly.

I am absolutely against the past.

Although Buddha tried in every way...but he was at the beginning point; you could not expect him to create the whole science of transcendence. He has my respect, my love – but I cannot tolerate to be compared with Gautam Buddha!

In fact, the government has to take action against this organization.

Gautam Buddha is an escapist, and it is Gautam Buddha who is responsible for the poverty of this country. If so many thousands of people renounce the world, they become parasites on the society.

I don't want you to renounce the world. My whole teaching is to rejoice in the world. What comparison can there be between me and Gautam Buddha?

Gautam Buddha is twenty-five centuries behind me. And as far as the allegation is concerned, that I have compared myself, it is an absolute lie!

This organization should understand that if even a little bit of Buddha's experience had been their experience, then this revengeful resolution asking the government to take action against me would not have happened. It does not show compassion, does not show meditation.

I want the government *not* to take any action against this organization. I, with all my friends, forgive them. The blind need forgiveness, the ignorant need compassion.

One thing should be understood definitively: I am a buddha in my own self – and the word 'buddha' is not the monopoly of anybody. It simply means the awakened one. It was not Gautam Buddha's name; his name was Gautam Siddharth. When he became awakened, those who understood his enlightenment started calling him Gautam Buddha.

But the word 'buddha', according to Gautam Buddha too, is simply the name of what is inherent in every human

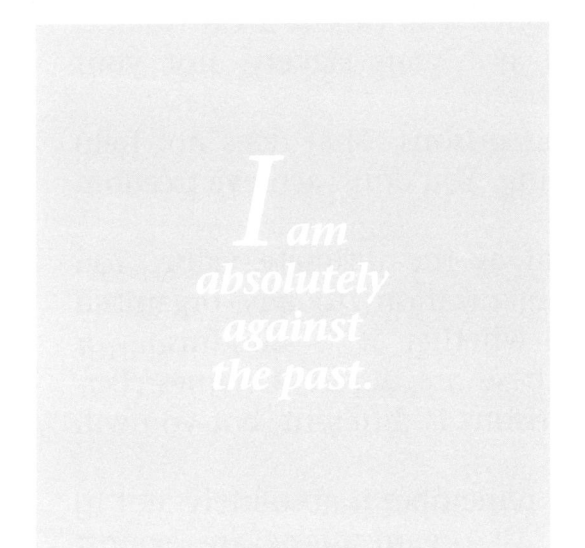

I am absolutely against the past.

being, and not only in every human being, but every living being. It is the intrinsic quality of everybody.

Everybody has the birthright to become a buddha.

These poor Buddhists don't understand at all the message of Gautam Buddha. How can they understand me? I have gone far beyond Gautam Buddha.

I have been teaching you all to be buddhas, but nobody has to be a Buddhist. To be a Buddhist is again falling into another prison. They have escaped from the Hindu fold, and now they have fallen into another fold. The names of the prisons are different, but you are a prisoner all the same. You were a Hindu, you were a prisoner; you can be a Christian... The prison will change, but not your slavery, not your consciousness.

People go on changing their prisons. That does not help any transformation in your being. You don't achieve freedom by changing prisons .

I teach my people freedom as the ultimate value. You should not belong to any organization, to any organized religion. It does not matter whether it is Buddhism, or Christianity, or Hinduism – these are different names. Perhaps the architecture of the prisons is different, but you will be a prisoner all the same.

Hence, I want my people to remember it absolutely, not to belong to any organization. All organizations are against individual freedom. And if there is no individual freedom, there is no possibility of spiritual growth.

You should stand on your own. You don't need any organization, any church, to transform you. You have all that is needed within you; you can be a buddha in your own right. That does not mean you are comparing yourself with

Gautam Buddha. Gautam Buddha is too backward.

And I have consistently said that Gautam Buddha is not a complete being, because in renouncing the outer, he has dropped one of his wings. Now he is flopping with one wing.

I want my people to have both the wings healthy. They are not against each other, they support each other. You cannot fly with one wing. You need two wings – the outer and the inner, the material and the spiritual, the visible and the invisible. Buddha is only half a man. I want you to be the whole man.

How can I compare myself with Gautam Buddha? I am a complete man! The outer world is my world, and the inner world is also my world, and I enjoy both, I love both. I love the flowers of the outer world, the rainbows, the dance of rains, the rivers, the mountains, the oceans. And at the same time I know my inner treasures, my inner ecstasies. And I don't see in them any contradiction.

You don't have to renounce anything, you don't have to choose anything. You have to be choicelessly aware of both: the outer and the inner. Rejoice in both, and your enrichment will be far greater than any Gautam Buddha.

On February 29, 1989 the disciples of Rajneesh collectively decided to call Him **Osho Rajneesh.**

OSHO is a term derived from ancient Japanese, and was first used by Eka, to address his master, Bodhidharma.

'**O**' means "with great respect, love and gratitude" as well as "synchronicity" and "harmony."

'**SHO**' means "multidimensional expansion of consciousness" and "existence showering from all directions."

BOOKS BY OSHO RAJNEESH
ENGLISH LANGUAGE EDITIONS

RAJNEESH PUBLISHERS

Early Discourses and Writings
A Cup of Tea *Letters to Disciples*
From Sex to Superconsciousness
I Am the Gate
The Long and the Short and the All
The Silent Explosion

Meditation
And Now, and Here (Volumes 1&2)
The Book of the Secrets (Volumes 1–5)
   Vigyana Bhairava Tantra
Dimensions Beyond the Known
In Search of the Miraculous (Volume 1)
Meditation: The Art of Ecstasy
Meditation: The First and Last Freedom
The Orange Book *The Meditation Techniques of Bhagwan Shree Rajneesh*
The Perfect Way
The Psychology of the Esoteric

Buddha and Buddhist Masters
The Book of the Books (Volumes 1–4)
   The Dhammapada
The Diamond Sutra *The Vajrachchedika Prajnaparamita Sutra*
The Discipline of Transcendence (Volumes 1–4)
   On the Sutra of 42 Chapters
The Heart Sutra
   The Prajnaparamita Hridayam Sutra
The Book of Wisdom (Volumes 1&2)
   Atisha's Seven Points of Mind Training

Indian Mystics:
The Bauls
The Beloved (Volumes 1&2)

Kabir
The Divine Melody
Ecstasy – The Forgotten Language
The Fish in the Sea is Not Thirsty
The Guest

The Path of Love
The Revolution

Krishna
Krishna: The Man and His Philosophy

Jesus and Christian Mystics
Come Follow Me (Volumes 1–4) *The Sayings of Jesus*
I Say Unto You (Volumes 1&2) *The Sayings of Jesus*
The Mustard Seed *The Gospel of Thomas*
Theologia Mystica *The Treatise of St. Dionysius*

Jewish Mystics
The Art of Dying
The True Sage

Sufism
Just Like That
Mojud, The Man with the Inexplicable Life
   Excerpts from The Wisdom of the Sands
The Perfect Master (Volumes 1&2)
The Secret
Sufis: The People of the Path (Volumes 1&2)
Unio Mystica (Volumes 1&2) *The Hadiqa of Hakim Sanai*
Until You Die
The Wisdom of the Sands (Volumes 1&2)

Tantra
Tantra, Spirituality and Sex *Excerpts from The Book of the Secrets*
Tantra: The Supreme Understanding
   Tilopa's Song of Mahamudra
The Tantra Vision (Volumes 1&2) *The Royal Song of Saraha*

Tao
The Empty Boat *The Stories of Chuang Tzu*
The Secret of Secrets (Volumes 1&2)
   The Secret of the Golden Flower
Tao: The Golden Gate (Volumes 1&2)
Tao: The Pathless Path (Vols. 1&2) *The Stories of Lieh Tzu*
Tao: The Three Treasures (Volumes 1–4)
   The Tao Te Ching of Lao Tzu
When the Shoe Fits *The Stories of Chuang Tzu*

The Upanishads

I Am That *Isa Upanishad*
Philosophia Ultima *Mandukya Upanishad*
The Supreme Doctrine *Kenopanishad*
That Art Thou *Sarvasar Upanishad, Kaivalya Upanishad, Adhyatma Upanishad*
The Ultimate Alchemy (Volumes 1&2) *Atma Pooja Upanishad*
Vedanta: Seven Steps to Samadhi *Akshya Upanishad*

Western Mystics

Guida Spirituale *On the Desiderata*
The Hidden Harmony *The Fragments of Heraclitus*
The Messiah (Volumes 1&2) *Commentaries on Kahlil Gibran's The Prophet*
The New Alchemy: To Turn You On *Mabel Collins' Light on the Path*
Philosophia Perennis (Volumes 1&2) *The Golden Verses of Pythagoras*
Zarathustra: A God That Can Dance *Commentaries on Friedrich Nietzsche's Thus Spoke Zarathustra*
Zarathustra: The Laughing Prophet *Commentaries on Friedrich Nietzsche's Thus Spoke Zarathustra*

Yoga

Yoga: The Alpha and the Omega (Volumess 1–10) *The Yoga Sutras of Patanjali*
Yoga: The Science of the Soul (Volumes 1–3) *Original Title: Yoga:The Alpha and the Omega (Volumes 1–3)*

Zen and Zen Masters

Poona 1974-1981

Ah, This!
Ancient Music in the Pines
And the Flowers Showered
Dang Dang Doko Dang
The First Principle
The Grass Grows By Itself
Hsin Hsin Ming: The Book of Nothing *Discourses on the Faith-Mind of Sosan*
Nirvana: The Last Nightmare
No Water, No Moon
Returning to the Source
Roots and Wings
The Search *The Ten Bulls of Zen*
A Sudden Clash of Thunder
The Sun Rises in the Evening
Take it Easy (Vols 1&2) *Poems of Ikkyu*
This Very Body the Buddha *Hakuin's Song of Meditation*
Walking in Zen, Sitting in Zen
The White Lotus *The Sayings of Bodhidharma*
Zen: The Path of Paradox (Volumes 1–3)
Zen: The Special Transmission

The Mystery School 1986-present

Bodhidharma The Greatest Zen Master *Commentaries on the Teachings of the Messenger of Zen from India to China*
Christianity: The Deadliest Poison and Zen: The Antidote to All Poisons
Communism and Zen Fire, Zen Wind
God is Dead Now Zen is the only Living Truth
The Great Zen Master Ta Hui *Reflections on the Transformation of an Intellectual to Enlightenment*
I Celebrate Myself God is No Where: Life is Now Here
Kyōzan: A True Man of Zen
No Mind: The Flowers of Eternity
The Zen Manifesto
Zen: The Mystery and the Poetry of the Beyond

The World of Zen *A boxed set of 5 volumes, containing:* *
 Live Zen
 This. This. A Thousand Times This.
 Zen: The Quantum Leap from Mind to No-Mind
 Zen: The Solitary Bird, Cuckoo of the Forest
 Zen: The Diamond Thunderbolt

Zen: All the Colors of the Rainbow
 A boxed set of 5 volumes, containing: *
 The Miracle
 Turning In
 The Original Man
 The Language of Existence
 The Buddha: The Emptiness of the Heart

Osho Rajneesh: The Present Day Awakened One Speaks on the Ancient Masters of Zen
 A boxed set of 7 volumes, containing: *
 Dōgen, the Zen Master: A Search and a Fulfillment
 Ma Tzu: The Empty Mirror
 Hyakujō: The Everest of Zen, with Bashō's Haikus
 Nansen: The Point of Departure
 Jōshū: The Lion's Roar
 Rinzai: Master of the Irrational
 Isan: No Footprints in the Blue Sky

Each volume is also available individually

Responses to Questions:
Poona 1974-1981

Be Still and Know
The Goose is Out!
My Way: The Way of the White Clouds
Walk Without Feet, Fly Without Wings
  and Think Without Mind
The Wild Geese and the Water
Zen: Zest, Zip, Zap and Zing

Rajneeshpuram

From Darkness to Light *Answers to the Seekers of the Path*
From the False to the Truth
  Answers to the Seekers of the Path
The Rajneesh Bible (Volumes 1–4)

The World Tour

Beyond Psychology *Talks in Uruguay*
Light on the Path *Talks in the Himalayas*
The Path of the Mystic *Talks in Uruguay*
Socrates Poisoned Again After 25 Centuries
  Talks in Greece
The Sword and the Lotus *Talks in the Himalayas*
The Transmission of the Lamp *Talks in Uruguay*

The Mystery School 1986-present

Beyond Enlightenment
The Golden Future
The Great Pilgrimage: From Here to Here
The Hidden Splendor
The Invitation
The New Dawn
The Rajneesh Upanishad
The Razor's Edge
The Rebellious Spirit
Sermons in Stones
YAA-HOO! The Mystic Rose

The Mantra Series:
  Satyam-Shivam-Sundram *Truth-Godliness-Beauty*
  Sat-Chit-Anand *Truth-Consciousness-Bliss*
  Om Mani Padme Hum *The Sound of Silence:*
    The Diamond in the Lotus
  Hari Om Tat Sat *The Divine Sound: That is the Truth*
  Om Shantih Shantih Shantih *The Soundless Sound:*
    Peace, Peace, Peace

Personal Glimpses

Books I Have Loved
Glimpses of a Golden Childhood
Notes of a Madman

Interviews with the World Press

The Last Testament (Volume 1)

Compilations

Beyond the Frontiers of the Mind
Bhagwan Shree Rajneesh
  On Basic Human Rights
The Book *An Introduction to the Teachings of*
  Bhagwan Shree Rajneesh
  Series I   from A – H
  Series II from I – Q
  Series III from R – Z
Death: The Greatest Fiction
Gold Nuggets
The Greatest Challenge: The Golden Future
I Teach Religiousness Not Religion
Jesus Crucified Again, This Time in
  Ronald Reagan's America
Life, Love, Laughter
More Gold Nuggets
More Words from a Man of No Words
The New Man: The Only Hope for the Future
A New Vision of Women's Liberation
Priests and Politicians: The Mafia of the Soul
The Rebel: The Very Salt of the Earth
Sex: Quotations from Bhagwan Shree Rajneesh
Words from a Man of No Words

Photobiographies

Shree Rajneesh: A Man of Many Climates, Seasons and
  Rainbows *Through the Eye of the Camera*
The Sound of Running Water *Bhagwan Shree Rajneesh*
  and His Work 1974–1978
This Very Place The Lotus Paradise *Bhagwan Shree*
  Rajneesh and His Work 1978–1984

Books about Osho Rajneesh

Bhagwan Shree Rajneesh: The Most Dangerous Man
  Since Jesus Christ *(by Sue Appleton, LL.B.)*
Bhagwan: The Buddha For The Future
  (by Juliet Forman, S.R.N., S.C.M., R.M.N.)
Bhagwan: The Most Godless Yet The Most Godly Man
  (by Dr. George Meredith M.D. M.B.,B.S. M.R.C.P.)
Bhagwan: Twelve Days That Shook The World
  (by Juliet Forman, S.R.N., S.C.M., R.M.N.)

Was Bhagwan Shree Rajneesh Poisoned By Ronald Reagan's America? *(by Sue Appleton, LL.B.)*

OTHER PUBLISHERS

UNITED KINGDOM

The Art of Dying *(Sheldon Press)*
The Book of the Secrets *(Volume 1, Thames & Hudson)*
Dimensions Beyond the Known *(Sheldon Press)*
The Hidden Harmony *(Sheldon Press)*
Meditation: The Art of Ecstasy *(Sheldon Press)*
The Mustard Seed *(Sheldon Press)*
Neither This Nor That *(Sheldon Press)*
No Water, No Moon *(Sheldon Press)*
Roots and Wings *(Routledge & Kegan Paul)*
Straight to Freedom *(Original title:
 Until You Die, Sheldon Press)*
The Supreme Understanding *(Original title:
 Tantra: The Supreme Understanding, Sheldon Press)*
The Supreme Doctrine *(Routledge & Kegan Paul)*
Tao: The Three Treasures *(Volume 1, Wildwood House)*

Books about Osho Rajneesh

The Way of the Heart: the Rajneesh Movement
 by Judith Thompson and Paul Heelas, Department of Religious Studies, University of Lancaster (Aquarian Press)

UNITED STATES OF AMERICA

And the Flowers Showered *(De Vorss)*
The Book of the Secrets *(Volumes 1–3, Harper & Row)*
Dimensions Beyond the Known
 (Wisdom Garden Books)
The Grass Grows By Itself *(De Vorss)*
The Great Challenge *(Grove Press)*
Hammer on the Rock *(Grove Press)*
I Am the Gate *(Harper & Row)*
Journey Toward the Heart *(Original title:
 Until You Die, Harper & Row)*
Meditation: The Art of Ecstasy *(Original title:
 Dynamics of Meditation, Harper & Row)*
The Mustard Seed *(Harper & Row)*
My Way: The Way of the White Clouds *(Grove Press)*
Nirvana: The Last Nightmare *(Wisdom Garden Books)*
Only One Sky *(Original title: Tantra:
 The Supreme Understanding, Dutton)*
The Psychology of the Esoteric *(Harper & Row)*
Roots and Wings *(Routledge & Kegan Paul)*
The Supreme Doctrine *(Routledge & Kegan Paul)*
When the Shoe Fits *(De Vorss)*
Words Like Fire *(Original title: Come Follow Me,
 Volume 1, Harper & Row)*

Books about Osho Rajneesh

The Awakened One: The Life and Work of Bhagwan
 Shree Rajneesh *by Vasant Joshi (Harper & Row)*
Dying for Enlightenment
 by Bernard Gunther (Harper & Row)
Rajneeshpuram and the Abuse of Power
 by Ted Shay, Ph.D. (Scout Creek Press)
Rajneeshpuram, the Unwelcome Society
 by Kirk Braun (Scout Creek Press)
The Rajneesh Story: The Bhagwan's Garden
 by Dell Murphy (Linwood Press, Oregon)

FOREIGN LANGUAGE EDITIONS

Chinese
I am the Gate (Woolin)

Danish
Bhagwan Shree Rajneesh Om
 Grundlaeggende Menneskerettigheder (Premo)
 Bhagwan Shree Rajneesh On Basic Human Rights
Hemmelighedernes Bog (Borgens)
 The Book of the Secrets (Volume 1)
Hu-Meditation Og Kosmisk Orgasme (Borgens)
 Hu-Meditation and Cosmic Orgasm, Danish edition only

Dutch
Bhagwan Shree Rajneesh Over de Rechten van de Mens
 (Rajneesh Publikaties Nederland) *Bhagwan Shree Rajneesh On Basic Human Rights*
Het Boek der Geheimen (Mirananda)
 The Book of the Secrets (Volumes 1–5)
Dood, de Laatste Illusie (Rajneesh Publikaties Nederland)
 Death: the Greatest Fiction
Drink Mij (Ankh-Hermes) *Come Follow Me (Volume 3)*
Geen Water, Geen Maan (Mirananda)
 No Water, No Moon (Volumes 1&2)
Gezaaid in Goede Aarde (Ankh-Hermes)
 Come Follow Me (Volume 2)
Heel Eenvoudig (Mirananda) *Just Like That*
Ik Ben de Poort (Ankh-Hermes) *I am the Gate*
Ik Ben de Zee Die Je Zoekt (Ankh-Hermes)
 Come Follow Me (Volume 4)
Leven, Liefde, Lachen (Rajneesh Publikaties Nederland)
 Life, Love, Laughter

Manifesto voor een Gouden Toekomst (Rajneesh Publikaties Nederland) *The Greatest Challenge: The Golden Future*
Meditatie: De Kunst van Innerlijke Extase (Mirananda) *Meditation: The Art of Inner Ecstasy*
Mijn Weg, De Weg van de Witte Wolke (Arcanum) *My Way: The Way of the White Clouds*
Het Mosterdzaad (Mirananda) *The Mustard Seed*
De Nieuwe Mens (Volume 1) (Zorn) *Compilation on The New Man, Relationships, Education, Health, Dutch edition only*
De Nieuwe Mens (Volume 2) (Altamira) *Excerpts from The Last Testament (Volume 1), Dutch edition only*
Een Nieuwe Visie op de Bevrijding van de Vrouw (Rajneesh Publikaties Nederland) *A New Vision of Women's Liberation*
Het Oranje Meditatieboek (Ankh-Hermes) *The Orange Book*
Priesters & Politici: De Maffia van de Ziel (Rajneesh Publikaties Nederland) *Priests & Politicians: The Mafia of the Soul*
Psychologie en Evolutie (Ankh-Hermes) *The Psychology of the Esoteric*
De Rebel, het Zout der Aarde (Rajneesh Publikaties Nederland) *The Rebel: The Very Salt of the Earth*
Tantra: Het Allerhoogste Inzicht (Ankh-Hermes) *Tantra: The Supreme Understanding*
Tantra, Spiritualiteit en Seks (Ankh-Hermes) *Tantra, Spirituality and Sex*
De Tantra Visie (Arcanum) *The Tantra Vision (Volumes 1&2)*
Tau (Ankh-Hermes) *Tao: The Three Treasures (Volume 1)*
Totdat Je Sterft (Ankh-Hermes) *Until You Die*
De Verborgen Harmonie (Mirananda) *The Hidden Harmony*
Volg Mij (Ankh-Hermes) *Come Follow Me (Volume 1)*
Zoeken naar de Stier (Ankh-Hermes) *The Search*

Books about Osho Rajneesh

Bhagwan, Krishnamurti, Jung *by Dr. J. Foudraine* (Ankh-Hermes)
Bhagwan… Notities van een Discipel *by Dr. J. Foudraine* (Ankh-Hermes)
Bhagwan Shree Rajneesh, een Introduktie *by Dr. J. Foudraine* (Ankh-Hermes)
Jaren van Voorbereiding *by Dr. J. Foudraine* (Altamira)
Oorspronkelijk Gezicht *by Dr. J. Foudraine* (Ambo)
Van Rome naar Poona *by Deva Siddhartha* (Arcanum)
Een Tuin der Lusten? Het rebelse tantrisme van Bhagwan en het nieuwe tijdperk *by Sietse Visser* (Mirananda)
Wie is van Licht? *by Dr. J. Foudraine* (Sijthoff)

Finnish

Oikeus elamaan (Leela RMC) *Bhagwan Shree Rajneesh On Basic Human Rights*

French

L'Eveil a la Conscience Cosmique (Dangles) *The Psychology of the Esoteric*
Je Suis la Porte (EPI) *I am the Gate*
Le Livre des Secrets (Albin Michel) *The Book of Secrets (Volume 1)*
Le Livre Orange (Roland Denniel) *The Orange Book*
La Meditation Dynamique (Dangles) *Meditation: The Art of Inner Ecstasy*
Mon Chemin, le Chemin des Nuages Blancs (Pathik) *My Way, the Way of the White Clouds*
La Mort, l'Ultime Illusion (Pathik) *Death: the Greatest Fiction*

German

Alchemie der Verwandlung (Lotos) *The True Sage*
Auf der Suche (Sambuddha) *The Search*
Bhagwan Shree Rajneesh: Ueber die Grundrechte des Menschen (Rajneesh Verlag) *Bhagwan Shree Rajneesh On Basic Human Rights*
Das Buch der Geheimnisse (Heyne) *The Book of the Secrets (Volume 1)*
Ekstase: Die vergessene Sprache (Herzschlag) *Ecstasy – The Forgotten Language*
Esoterische Psychologie (Sannyas) *The Psychology of the Esoteric*
Der Freund (Sannyas Verlag) *A Cup of Tea*
Die Gans ist raus! (Rajneesh Verlag) *The Goose Is Out!*
Goldene Augenblicke: Portrait einer Jugend in Indien (Goldmann) *Glimpses of a Golden Childhood*
Gold Nuggets (Tao)
Die grösste Herausforderung: Die Goldene Zukunft (Rajneesh Verlag) *The Greatest Challenge: The Golden Future*
Der Höhepunkt des Lebens (Rajneesh Verlag) *Compilation on death, German edition only*
Ich bin der Weg (Sannyas) *I am the Gate*
Intelligenz des Herzens (Herzschlag) *Compilation, German edition only*
Jesus aber schwieg (Sannyas) *Come Follow Me (Volume 2)*

Jesus – der Menschensohn (Sannyas)
Come Follow Me (Volume 3)
Kein Wasser, Kein Mond (Herzschlag)
No Water, No Moon
Das Klatschen der einen Hand (Gyandip)
The Sound of One Hand Clapping
Komm und folge mir (Sannyas/Droemer Knaur)
Come Follow Me (Volume 1)
Kunst kommt nicht vom Können (Rajneesh Verlag)
Compilation about creativity, German edition only
Liebe beginnt nach den Flitterwochen (Rajneesh Verlag)
Compilation about love, German edition only
Meditation: Die Kunst, zu sich selbst zu finden (Heyne)
Meditation: The Art of Inner Ecstasy
Mein Rezept: Leben, Liebe, Lachen (Rajneesh Verlag)
Life, Love, Laughter
Mein Weg: Der Weg der weissen Wolke (Tao)
My Way: The Way of the White Clouds
Mit Wurzeln und Flügeln (Lotos) *Roots and Wings (Vol. 1)*
Nicht bevor du stirbst (Gyandip) *Until You Die*
Nirvana: Die letzte Hürde auf dem Weg
   (Rajneesh Verlag/NSI) *Nirvana: The Last Nightmare*
Das Orangene Buch (Rajneesh Verlag/NSI)
The Orange Book
Priester & Politiker – Die Mafia der Seele (Rajneesh Verlag)
Priests & Politicians: The Mafia of the Soul
Rebellion der Seele (Sannyas) *The Great Challenge*
Die Schuhe auf dem Kopf (Lotos) *Roots and Wings*
Sexualität und Aids (Rajneesh Verlag) *Compilation about AIDS, German edition only*
Spirituelle Entwicklung und Sexualität (Fischer)
Spiritual Development & Sexuality, German edition only
Sprengt den Fels der Unbewußtheit (Fischer)
Hammer on the Rock
Sprung ins Unbekannte (Sannyas)
Dimensions Beyond the Known
Tantra: Die höchste Einsicht (Sannyas)
Tantra: The Supreme Understanding
Tantra, Spiritualität und Sex (Rajneesh Verlag)
Tantra, Spirituality and Sex
Tantrische Liebeskunst (Sannyas)
Tantra, Spirituality and Sex
Tantrische Vision (Heyne) *The Tantra Vision (Volume 1)*
Das Ultimatum: Der Neue Mensch oder globaler
   Selbstmord (Rajneesh Verlag)
The New Man: The Only Hope for the Future
Und vor Allem: Nicht Wackeln! (Fachbuchhandlung für
   Psychologie) *Above All Don't Wobble*
Die verborgene Harmonie (Sannyas)
The Hidden Harmony
Die verbotene Wahrheit (Rajneesh Verlag/Heyne)
The Mustard Seed
Vom Sex zum kosmischen Bewußtsein
   (New Age/Thomas Martin)
From Sex to Superconsciousness
Was ist Meditation? (Sannyas) *Compilation about meditation, German edition only*
Worte eines Mannes ohne Worte (Rajneesh Verlag)
Words From A Man Of No Words
Yoga: Alpha und Omega (Gyandip)
Yoga: The Alpha and the Omega (Volume 1)
Die Zukunft gehört den Frauen – Neue
   Dimensionen der Frauenbefreiung (Rajneesh Verlag)
A New Vision of Women's Liberation

Books about Osho Rajneesh
Bhagwan: Gauner – Gaukler – Gott?
   by Fritz Tanner (Panorama)
Das Meisterstück *by Nisha Jacobi* (Context)
Der Erwachte – Leben und Werk von Bhagwan
   Shree Rajneesh *by Vasant Joshi* (Synthesis)
The Awakened One
Ganz entspannt im Hier und Jetzt – Tagebuch meines
   Lebens mit Bhagwan in Poona
   by Satyananda (Rowohlt)
Jesus – Bhagwan: ein Vergleich
   by Peter Preskill (Ahriman)
Im Grunde ist alles ganz einfach *by Satyananda* (Ullstein)

Greek
Bhagwan Shree Rajneesh Gia Ta Vasika Anthropina
   Dikeomata (Swami Anand Ram)
Bhagwan Shree Rajneesh On Basic Human Rights
I Krifi Armonia (PIGI/Rassoulis) *The Hidden Harmony*

Hebrew
Tantra: Ha'havana Ha'eelaeet (Massada)
Tantra: The Supreme Understanding

Italian
L'Armonia Nascosta (ECIG) *The Hidden Harmony*
Bagliori di un'Infanzia Dorata (Mediterranee)
Glimpses of a Golden Childhood
Bhagwan Shree Rajneesh parla sui Diritti dell'Uomo
   (Rajneesh Services Corporation)
Bhagwan Shree Rajneesh On Basic Human Rights
La Bibbia di Rajneesh (Bompiani)
The Rajneesh Bible (Volume 1)
Dal Sesso all'Eros Cosmico (Basaia)
From Sex to Superconsciousness

Dieci Storie Zen di Bhagwan Shree Rajneesh: Né Acqua,
  Né Luna (Mediterranee) *No Water, No Moon*
Dimensioni Oltre il Conosciuto (Mediterranee)
  Dimensions Beyond the Known
La Dottrina Suprema (Rizzoli) *The Supreme Doctrine*
Estasi: Il Linguaggio Dimenticato (Riza Libri)
  Ecstasy: The Forgotten Language
La Grande Sfida (SugarCo) *The Greatest Challenge:
  The Golden Future*
Guida Spirituale (Mondadori) *Guida Spirituale*
Io Sono la Soglia (Mediterranee) *I am the Gate*
Libri che Ho Amato (Rajneesh Services
  Corporation/Macro) *Books I Have Loved*
Il Libro Arancione (Mediterranee) *The Orange Book*
Il Libro dei Segreti (Bompiani)
  The Book of The Secrets (Volume 1)
Meditazione Dinamica: L'Arte dell'Estasi Interiore
  (Mediterranee) *Meditation: The Art of Inner Ecstasy*
La Mia Via: La Via delle Nuvole Bianche (Mediterranee)
  My Way: The Way of the White Clouds
Mojud: L'Uomo dalla Vita Inesplicabile
  (Rajneesh Services Corporation)
  Mojud: The Man With the Inexplicable Life
Nirvana: L'Ultimo Incubo (Basaia)
  Nirvana: The Last Nightmare
La Nuova Alchimia (Psiche)
  The New Alchemy To Turn You On
L'Oca È Fuori (Rajneesh Services Corporation)
  The Goose is Out!
Philosofia Perennis (ECIG)
  Philosophia Perennis (Volumes 1&2)
I Preti e I Politici – la Mafia dell'Anima
  (Rajneesh Services Corporation)
  Priests and Politicians: The Mafia of the Soul
Il Ribelle: Sale della Terra (Rajneesh Services Corporation)
  The Rebel: The Very Salt of the Earth
La Ricerca (La Salamandra) *The Search*
La Rivoluzione Interiore (Mediterranee)
  The Psychology of the Esoteric
Il Seme della Ribellione (ECIG) *The Mustard Seed*
Semi di Saggezza (Sugarco) *Seeds of Revolution*
Tantra: La Comprensione Suprema (Bompiani)
  Tantra: The Supreme Understanding
Tantra, Spiritualità e Sesso (Rajneesh Foundation Italy)
  Tantra, Spirituality and Sex
Tao: I Tre Tesori (Re Nudo)
  Tao: The Three Treasures (Volumes 1–3)
Tecniche di Liberazione (La Salamandra)
  Techniques of Liberation, Italian edition only
La Visione Tantrica (Riza) *The Tantra Vision*

Books about Osho Rajneesh
L'Incanto d'Arancio *by Svatantra Sarjano* (Savelli)

Japanese
Anata ga Shinumadewa (Fumikura) *Until You Die*
Ai no Renkinjutsu (Merkmal) *The Mustard Seed*
Baul no Ai no Uta (Merkmal) *The Beloved (Volumes 1&2)*
Bhagwan Shree Rajneesh Za Buddha Lodo Maitoreya
  (Meisosha Ltd.) *Compilation on Bhagwan the Buddha
  Lord Maitreya*
Diamond Sutra – Bhagwan Shree Rajneesh
  Kongohannyakyo o Kataru (Meisosha Ltd./LAF Mitsuya)
  The Diamond Sutra
Hannya Shinkyo (Merkmal) *The Heart Sutra*
Ikkyu Doka (Merkmal) *Take it Easy (Volumes 1 & 2)*
Kokuu no Fune (Rajneesh Enterprise Japan)
  The Empty Boat
Kusa wa hitorideni haeru (Fumikura)
  The Grass Grows by Itself
Kyukyoku no Tabi (Merkmal) *The Search*
Meiso – Shukusai no Art (Merkmal)
  Meditation: The Art of Inner Ecstasy
My Way – Nagareyuku Shirakumo no Michi (Rajneesh
  Publications) *My Way: The Way of the White Clouds*
Nyu Uman Tanjo (Rajneesh Enterprise Japan)
  A New Vision of Women's Liberation
Ooinaru Chousen – Ougon No Mirai
  The Greatest Challenge: The Golden Future (Rajneesh
  Enterprise Japan)
Ougon no Yōnenki (Rajneesh Enterprise Japan)
  Glimpses of a Golden Childhood
Orange Book (Wholistic Therapy Institute)
  The Orange Book
Seimei no Kanki (Rajneesh Enterprise Japan)
  Dance Your Way to God
Sex kara Choishiki e (Rajneesh Enterprise Japan)
  From Sex to Superconsciousness
Shin Jinkensengen (Meisosha Ltd.)
  Bhagwan Shree Rajneesh On Basic Human Rights
Sinshinmei (Zen Culture Institute)
  Hsin Hsin Ming – The Book of Nothing
Sonzai no Uta (Merkmal)
  Tantra: The Supreme Understanding
Tao: Eien no Taiga (Merkmal)
  Tao: The Three Treasures (Volumes 1–4)
Tamashii eno Hanzai (EER)
  Priests and Politicians: The Mafia of the Soul

Korean
Giromnun Gil II (Chung Ha)

Giromnun Gil Ih (Chung Ha)
  Tao: The Pathless Path (Volume 1)
Haeng Bongron Il
Haeng Bongron Ih
  Tao: The Pathless Path (Volume 2)
Joogumui Yesool (Chung Ha)   *The Art of Dying*
The Divine Melody (Chung Ha)
The Divine Melody (Sung Jung)
Salmuigil Hingurumui Gil (Chung Ha)   *The Empty Boat*
Seon (Chung Ha)   *The Grass Grows by Itself*
Upanishad (Chung Ha)   *Vedanta: Seven Steps to Samadhi*
Sesoggwa Chowol (Chung Ha)   *Roots and Wings*
Sinbijuijaui Norae (Chung Ha)   *The Revolution*
Mahamudraui Norae (Il Ghi Sa)
  Tantra: The Supreme Understanding
Sarahaui Norae (Il Ghi Sa)   *The Tantra Vision*
Meongsang Bibob (Il Ghi Sa)   *The Book of the Secrets*
Banya Simgeong (Il Ghi Sa)   *The Heart Sutra*
Kabir Meongsangsi (Il Ghi Sa)   *The Path of Love*
Salmui Choom Chimmoogui Choom (Kha Chee)
  Tao: The Three Treasures (Volumes 1–3)
Sarangui Yeongum Sool (Kim Young Sa)
  The Mustard Seed
Yeogieh Sala (Kim Young Sa)   *I am the Gate*
The Psychology of the Esoteric (Han Bat)
Soomun Johwa (Hong Sung Sa)   *The Hidden Harmony*
I Say Unto You (Hong Sung Sa)
Sunggwa Meongsang
From Sex to Superconsciousness (Sim Sul Dang)
From Sex to Superconsciousness (Ul Ghi)
The White Lotus (Jin Young)
Beshakaui Achim (Je Il)
  My Way: The Way of the White Clouds
Iroke Nanun Durotda (Je Il)   *The Diamond Sutra*
Meong Sang (Han Ma Um Sa)
  Meditation: The Art of Inner Ecstasy
The Orange Book (Gum Moon Dang)
Jameso Khaeonara (Bum Woo Sa)
The Search – The Ten Bulls of Zen
The Teaching of the Soul (Compilation) (Jeong-Um)
Alpha Grigo Omega (Jeong-Um)
  Yoga: The Alpha and the Omega (Volume 1)
Come Follow Me (Chung-Ha)
Philosophia Perennis (Chung-Ha)
Sinsim Meong (Hong-Bub)
  Hsin Hsin Ming: The Book of Nothing
Maumuro Ganungil (Moon Hak Sa Sang Sa)
  Journey towards the Heart
Saeroun Inganui Heong Meong   *Neo Tantra*
Hayan Yeonkhot   *The White Lotus*

Books about Osho Rajneesh
Jigum Yeogiyeso (Je Il)   *The Awakened One*

Polish
(Titles translated and available) *The Goose is Out!*
The Last Testament (Volume 1, Discourse 14)
The Mustard Seed
The Orange Book
The Rajneesh Bible (Volume 1,
  Discourses 1,4,6,13,16,20,28,29,30)
The Rajneesh Bible (Volume 2, Discourses 11,12,16)
The Rajneesh Upanishad (Discourses 2,16,40)
The Wild Geese and the Water (Discourse 1)
Medytacja Sztuka Ekstazy, Volume 1
  Meditation: The Art of Inner Ecstasy (Part 1)

Portuguese
Arte de Morrer (Global)   *The Art of Dying*
Cipreste No Jardim (Cultrix)
  The Cypress in the Courtyard
Dimensões Além do Conhecido (Cultrix)
  Dimensions Beyond the Known
A Divina Melodia (Cultrix)   *The Divine Melody*
A Nova Criança (ECO, Brasil)   *The New Child*
Do Sexo A Superconsciência (Cultrix)
  From Sex to Superconsciousness
Eu Sou A Porta (Pensamento)   *I am the Gate*
Êxtase: A Linguagem Esquecida (Global)
  Ecstasy – The Forgotten Language
A Harmonia Oculta (Pensamento)   *The Hidden Harmony*
O Livro Dos Segredos (Maha Lakshmi)
  The Book of the Secrets (Volumes 1&2)
O Livro Orange (Pensamento)   *The Orange Book*
O Novo Homem: A Única Esperança Para O Futuro
  The New Man: The Only Hope For The Future
Meditação: A Arte Do Êxtase (Cultrix)   *Meditation:*
  The Art of Inner Ecstasy
Meu Caminho: O Caminho Das Nuvens Brancas (Tao)
  My Way: The Way of the White Clouds
Nem Agua, Nem Lua (Pensamento)   *No Water, No Moon*
Notas De Um Homem Louco (NAIM)
  Notes of a Madman
A Nova Alquimia (Cultrix)
  The New Alchemy: To Turn You On
Uma Nova Visão sobre a Liberação da Mulher (Abhudaya)
  A New Vision of Women's Liberation
Palavras De Fogo (Global/Ground)
  Come Follow Me (Volume 1)
A Psicologia Do Esotérico (Tao)
  The Psychology of the Esoteric

Raízes E Asas (Cultrix) *Roots and Wings*
A Semente De Mostarda (Tao)
   The Mustard Seed (Volumes 1&2)
Sobre Os Direitos Humanos Basicos (Naim)
   Bhagwan Shree Rajneesh On Basic Human Rights
Sufis: O Povo do Caminho (Maha
   Lakshmi) *Sufis: The People of the Path*
Tantra, Sexo E Espiritualidade (Agora)
   Tantra, Spirituality and Sex
Tantra: A Suprema Compreensão (Cultrix)
   Tantra: The Supreme Understanding
Unio Mystica (Maha Lakshmi) *Unio Mystica*

Russian

Bhagwan Shree Rajneesh On Basic Human Rights
   (Neo-Sannyas International)
Titles translated and available:
The Book of the Secrets, Volume 1
Dimensions Beyond the Known
I am the Gate
Meditation: The Art of Inner Ecstasy
The Mustard Seed
Neither This nor That
Nirvana: The Last Nightmare
The Psychology of the Esoteric
Roots and Wings
The Sound of One Hand Clapping
Straight to Freedom
The Supreme Doctrine
Tantra: The Supreme Understanding
Tao: The Three Treasures
This is It
The White Lotus

Serbo-Croat

Bhagwan Shree Rajneesh (Swami Mahavira)
   Compilation of various quotations
Novo Videnje Oslobodenja Zene (Swami Mahavira)
   A New Vision of Women's Liberation
The Ultimate Pilgrimage
Vrovno Hodocasce *A Rajneesh Reader*
Bhagwan Shree Rajneesh O Osnovnim Pravima Covjeka
   Bhagwan Shree Rajneesh On Basic Human Rights

Spanish

El Arbol del Amor (Gulaab, Spain) *The Tree of Love*
   (Bilingual – Excerpts from:
   From Sex to Superconsciousness)
El Camino de las Nubes Blancas (Cuatro Vientos, Chile)
   My Way: The Way of the White Clouds
Celebra! Medita! (Padma RMC, Columbia)
   Celebrate! Meditate!, Spanish edition only
Del Sexo a la Superconsciencia (Gulaab, Spain)
   From Sex to Superconsciousness
El Hombre de Vida Inexplicable (Gulaab, Spain)
   Mojud, the Man with the Inexplicable Life
Introducción al Mundo del Tantra (Roselló Impresiones,
   Spain) *Tantra: The Supreme Understanding*
El Libro Naranja (Bhagwatam, Puerto Rico)
   The Orange Book
Y Llovieron Flores (Barath, Spain)
   And the Flowers Showered
El Major Desafío: El Futuro de Oro (Gulaab, Spain)
   The Greatest Challenge: The Golden Future
Meditación: El Arte del Extasis (Roselló Impresiones,
   Spain) *Meditation: The Art of Inner Ecstasy*
Muerte: la Mayor Ficción (Gulaab, Spain)
   Death: The Greatest Fiction
Nuevo Hombre: La Unica Esperanza del Futuro
   (Nartano, Puerto Rico)
   The New Man: The Only Hope For The Future
Psicologia de lo Esotérico: La Nueva Evolución del Hombre
   (Cuatro Vientos, Chile) *The Psychology of the Esoteric*
Que Es Meditación? (Koan/Roselló Pastanaga, Spain)
   What Is Meditation?
El Rebelde, La Sal de la Tierra (Barath, Spain)
   The Rebel: The Very Salt of the Earth
Sacerdotes y Políticos: La Mafia del Alma (Gulaab, Spain)
   Priests And Politicians: The Mafia Of The Soul
Sobre Los Derechos Humanos Básicos (Futonia, Spain)
   Bhagwan Shree Rajneesh On Basic Human Rights
Solo Un Cielo (Collection Tantra, Spain)
   Tantra: The Supreme Understanding
El Sutra del Corazón (Sarvogeet, Spain) *The Heart Sutra*
Tao: Los Tres Tesoros (Sirio, Spain)
   Tao: The Three Treasures
Una Nueva Visión sobre la Liberación de la Mujer
   (Gulaab, Spain) *A New Vision of Women's Liberation*
Ven, Sígueme (Sagaró, Chile)
   Come Follow Me (Volume 1)
Vida, Amor y Risa (Gulaab, Spain) *Life, Love, Laughter*
Yo Soy La Puerta (Diana, Mexico) *I am The Gate*

Swedish

Den Vaeldiga Utmaningen (Livskraft)
   The Great Challenge

WORLDWIDE DISTRIBUTION CENTERS FOR THE WORKS OF OSHO RAJNEESH

EUROPE

Belgium
Indu Rajneesh Meditation Center
Coebergerstr. 40
2018 Antwerpen
Tel.   3/237 2037
Fax   3/216 9871

Denmark
Anwar Distribution
Carl Johansgade 8, 5
2100 Copenhagen
Tel.   01/420 218
Fax   01/147 348

Finland
Unio Mystica Shop for Meditative Books & Tapes
Albertinkatu 10
P.O. Box 186
00121 Helsinki
Tel.   3580/665 811

Italy
Rajneesh Services Corporation
Via XX Settembre 12
28041 Arona (NO)
Tel.   02/839 2194 (Milan office)
Fax   02/832 3683

Netherlands
Rajneesh Distributie Centrum
Cornelis Troostplein 23
1072 JJ Amsterdam
Tel.   020/5732 130
Fax   020/5732 132

Norway
Devananda Rajneesh Meditation Center
P.O. Box 177 Vinderen
0319 Oslo 3
Tel.   02/491 590

Spain
Distribuciones "El Rebelde"
Estellencs
07192 Mallorca - Baleares
Tel.   71/410 470
Fax   71/719 027

Sweden
Madhur Rajneesh Meditation Center
Nidalvsgrand 15
12161 Johanneshov / Stockholm
Tel.   08/394 996
Fax   08/184 972

Switzerland
Mingus Rajneesh Meditation Center
Asylstrasse 11
8032 Zurich
Tel.   01/2522 012

United Kingdom
Purnima Rajneesh
Centre for Meditation
Spring House, Spring Place
London NW5 3BH
Tel.   01/284 1415
Fax   01/267 1848

West Germany
The Rebel Publishing House GmbH*
Venloer Strasse 5-7
5000 Cologne 1
Tel.   0221/574 0742
Fax   0221/574 0749
*All books available AT COST PRICE

Rajneesh Verlag GmbH
Venloer Strasse 5-7
5000 Cologne 1
Tel.   0221/574 0743
Fax   0221/574 0749

Tao Institut
Klenzestrasse 41
8000 Munich 5
Tel.   089/201 6657
Fax   089/201 3056

AUSTRALIA
Rajneesh Meditation & Healing Centre
P.O. Box 1097
160 High Street
Fremantle, WA 6160
Tel.   09/430 4047
Fax   09/384 8557

AMERICA
United States

Chidvilas
P.O. Box 17550
Boulder, CO 80308
Tel.   303/665 6611
Fax   303/665 6612
Order Dept. 800/777 7743

Ansu Publishing Co., Inc.
19023 SW Eastside Rd
Lake Oswego,
OR 97034
Tel.   503/638 5240
Fax   503/638 5101

Nartano
P.O. Box 51171
Levittown,
Puerto Rico 00950-1171
Tel. 809/795 8829

Also available in bookstores nationwide at Walden Books

Canada

Publications Rajneesh
P.O. Box 331
Outremont, QUE. H2V 4N1
Tel.   514/276 2680

ASIA
India

Sadhana Foundation*
17 Koregaon Park
Poona 411 001, MS
Tel.   0212/660 963
Fax   0212/664 181
*All books available AT COST PRICE

Japan

Eer Rajneesh Neo-Sannyas Commune
Mimura Building 6-21-34
Kikuna, Kohoku-ku
Yokohama, 222
Tel.   045/434 1981
Fax   045/434 5565

RAJNEESH MEDITATION CENTERS ASHRAMS AND COMMUNES

There are many Rajneesh Meditation Centers throughout the world which can be contacted for information about the teachings of Osho Rajneesh and which have His books available as well as audio and video tapes of His discourses. Centers exist in practically every country.

FOR FURTHER INFORMATION ABOUT OSHO RAJNEESH

Rajneeshdham Neo-Sannyas Commune
17 Koregaon Park
Poona 411 001, MS
India

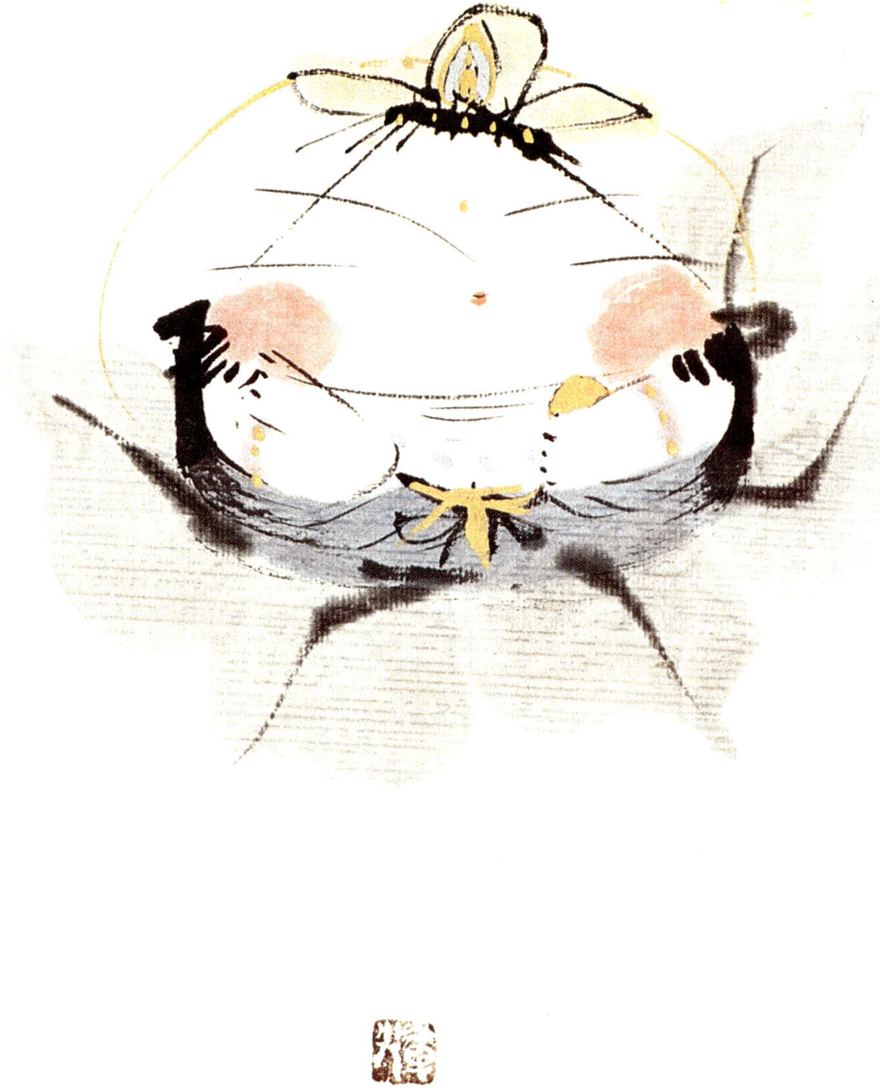

THE GREAT SWAN
ON THE WING;
THE FLIGHT
OF THE ALONE
TO THE ALONE.